Praise for
The Little Black Book of Online Business

This "Little Black Book" is a must-have reference for everyone already doing business online or anyone who wants to. Instead of haphazardly bookmarking a few pages here and there, Paul has given you 1,001 (actually more) critical resources for all aspects of success in your online businesses. I suggest you keep it close to your computer at all times!

—Yanik Silver
InternetLifestyle.com

Saves you hours of boring research . . . and the painful costs of trial-and-error . . . the singular guide to finding anything you need to grow your online business. This is a must-have resource for anyone who does business on the Internet!

—Ray Edwards,
Internationally-known copywriter
and marketing strategist,
RayEdwards.com

Wow—what a terrific, must-have resource your book is. From now on, it's one of the first places I'll turn when I need to get something done for my business.

—David Deutsch,
Renowned direct response copywriter,
copyquickstart.com

One of the fastest ways to boost your profits is to find better vendors who'll do a better job at a lower price than the ones you're using now, while saving you time and aggravation. This book is full of such companies and my guess is it'll pay for itself 1,000 times over when you find just one good resource. Highly recommended.

—Bill Harrison, Partner
FreePublicity.com

Paul Galloway is one of the few business people I know who puts the interests of his clients and customers ahead of his own. This selfless collection of resources is no exception, and should help anyone get more done online, faster and easier.

—Tim Gross, Educated Media LLC
TimGross.com

Wearing a lot of 'hats' in our online business, it's awesome to have a resource like this at my fingertips—it's a must-have for anyone working in an online business.

—Melissa Feiveson
SurefireMarketing.com

The
LITTLE BLACK BOOK
of
ONLINE BUSINESS

1001
INSIDER RESOURCES
EVERY
BUSINESS OWNER
NEEDS

Paul Galloway

WILEY

John Wiley & Sons, Inc.

Published by John Wiley & Sons, Inc., Hoboken, New Jersey.
Published simultaneously in Canada.

For general information on our other products and services or for technical support, please contact our Customer Care Department within the United States at (800) 762-2974, outside the United States at (317) 572-3993 or fax (317) 572-4002.

Wiley also publishes its books in a variety of electronic formats. Some content that appears in print may not be available in electronic books. For more information about Wiley products, visit our web site at www.wiley.com.

Library of Congress Cataloging-in-Publication Data:

Galloway, Paul.
    The little black book of online business : 1001 insider resources every business owner needs / Paul Galloway.
        p.   cm.
    Includes index.
    ISBN 978-0-470-40776-9 (cloth)
        1.   Electronic commerce—Handbooks, manuals, etc.   I. Title.
HF5548.32.G355   2009
658.8'72—dc22
                                                                        2008037337

Printed in the United States of America

10   9   8   7   6   5   4   3   2   1

To my sweet wife, LaRae. As I sat in my quiet office writing this book, you managed our four young and energetic children—and you voiced not a single complaint. You are an extraordinary woman, and I'm lucky to have you.

Contents

Foreword

These days, business recommendations are often given out thoughtlessly, like candies to patients in a waiting room.

If you ask someone to endorse your book or to recommend your product, often such requests are considered with self-serving interests in mind:

> "If I endorse that book my profile will go up with the sales of the book."
>
> "If I recommend this product I'll earn a commission."

The one thing that generally isn't considered is the impact such a recommendation will have on the recipient.

If the people making these recommendations truly understood, they wouldn't give them out so lightly.

A single recommendation from a perceived authority figure can send the arc of someone's life heading off into a totally different direction. Shouldn't those wielding this power do so with a bit of responsibility?

Heck, when thought of like this, calling such responsibility a "sacred trust" isn't too far of a stretch.

I've known Paul Galloway for many years now, and not only has he proven himself to be a formidably adept business expert, but also a supremely trustworthy one. He has a rare combination of technical and marketing knowledge that makes him uniquely qualified to write this book.

But still . . . when I heard about this book I had an immediate reaction of skepticism.

I remember a similar book being offered in recent memory that was nothing but a self-serving collection of commissioned recommendations for shoddy services. Heck, many such "books" exist—especially in the online business world, I'm sad to say.

When I opened the *Little Black Book* for the first time, though, I simply couldn't put it down for a full hour. I loved it so much that I immediately offered to introduce him to my publisher. Obviously, that's not a favor I would do for just any book, lest I wear out that welcome. (Smart tacticians don't fire their most powerful weapon freely—only when it counts.)

Paul has taken this sacred trust quite seriously and brings to you a collection of resources that can shave the equivalent of a year's time off the learning curve of your business.

One of the most frustrating parts of starting a business online is knowing who to trust. The Internet, as I write this, is widely unregulated and, by god, I hope it stays that way. But like any unregulated market, it has its share of rogues and traps.

Paul has put together a series of signposts that will help you to navigate safely through that mess.

Where will those signposts lead?

Well, that's totally up to you.

Will you start a small business that brings in a bit of cash to put your kids through school or to buy that boat?

Maybe you'll start a web site that makes you the champion of your favorite cause?

Or maybe you'll create the next Google?

Chances are someone reading this foreword will be all of those things.

Why not you?

Mark Joyner
Author of *The Irresistible Offer*

Introduction

So, you want to take your business online?

>Should you use a shared server for hosting your web site, or a dedicated server?
>
>Who will your hosting company be?
>
>How about your:
>
>>E-mail solution?
>>
>>Sequential autoresponder service?
>>
>>Help desk software?
>
>And once your site is built, how are you going to get people to visit?
>
>What other online resources are available to help you grow your business?

This book answers those questions and points you to the online business tools that will give you an advantage in the marketplace.

Not only will you find some of the best resources for tools you've already heard about, but you'll find many tools you didn't even know existed!

Rather than organizing this guide as a typical book with chapters, I have elected to list the various resources alphabetically by function—I believe this is a more intuitive and usable approach.

Though I include *many* links/resources relevant to these topics, this book is not an Internet promotion or web site design how-to. Likewise, it's not a how-to-make-money-on-the-Internet or a doing-business-on-the-Internet book.

This guide will give you the *tools* to implement just about any marketing program online—but you'll have to come up with the business idea yourself.

A few words about the various resources I link to in this guide . . .

These links are not listed in any particular order within a category. A resource listed first in a category is not necessarily any better than the resource listed last in that same category.

These links are not (could never be!) all-inclusive. I have purposely omitted some resources for one or more of the following reasons:

High price (if there were viable alternatives at lower cost)
Couldn't find price
Questionable ethics
Too much hype
Already have several similar resources

I've also avoided the inclusion of how-to e-books, courses, guides, and so on, with a few notable exceptions.

I have sifted through thousands of links/resources before settling on the ones here. I have tried my best to include only resources from reputable companies offering good value for the money. I have often relied on the recommendations of other online business owners I know. In some cases, the recommendations have come from researching the related user forums.

However, since I haven't personally used *all* of these services (many, but not all), their inclusion here does not constitute a personal endorsement or guarantee on my part. It is still your responsibility to check out each resource of interest for yourself and make sure it's a good fit with your needs.

Why didn't I just include the very best choice in each category? Different people reading this book will have different needs, and my favorite company for a given type of service could well be the worst choice for someone else. So I have included multiple choices when possible—I believe they're all good, but which one works best for you is a question only you can answer.

The Internet is a very dynamic place, and links change frequently. In many cases, I have linked directly to a specific product/service of a company rather than to its home page.

It's quite likely that a number of these pages, over time, will be moved to other places on the company site. If you try a link and get a "file not found" message, try "backing up." To illustrate, suppose you tried this link:

http://www.example.com/products/thisproduct

If the link yielded a "file not found" error, the next thing you should try is this:

http://www.example.com/products

This page would very likely contain a listing of the various products sold. If *that* doesn't work, then your final option is to try the company's home page:

http://www.example.com/

Unless the company has folded completely, this page should include links to its "products," "services," "solutions," and so forth.

I make no commissions on any of the links in this book.

Some of these links are duplicated in different categories, because they apply to both. For instance, many companies that do CD duplication also offer fulfillment services. At last count, the total number of *unique* links was 1,229.

Because things change so rapidly online, I have created a web site just for owners of this book. Please enter this web address in your browser:

http://www.LittleBlackBookRewards.com/

Registration is free and will give you access to additional resource links, free downloadable software, and more.

HOW TO USE THIS BOOK . . .

If you have an immediate specific need, then just look up that topic (and/or related topics) in the contents and go directly to the corresponding pages in the guide.

I believe you will discover a number of useful (and previously unknown) resources just by browsing the contents and turning to the pages of interest—or by scanning the guide from cover to cover.

I'm certain your introduction to some of these resources will also trigger marketing ideas you hadn't thought of before. Let's get to it!

The
LITTLE BLACK BOOK
of
ONLINE BUSINESS

Advertising

Getting people to identify themselves as interested in your product is the critical first step of your marketing efforts. Advertising is what brings them into your sales funnel, and everything after that is more generally classified as marketing.

Advertising can be simplified as a three-step process:

1. Identify the people for whom your product holds the most appeal.
2. Determine where on the Internet these people are likely to be found.
3. Put your lead-generation advertising in front of them in those places.

With the Internet, all three of these steps can be accomplished in an astonishingly short time frame—I'm talking *hours* instead of weeks or months!

What's more, the Internet gives you the power to accurately measure the effectiveness of your advertising. You can measure the number of visitors from each advertising source, cost per visitor, revenue per visitor, and most important, your ROI.

This level of advertising accountability allows you to quickly terminate the "losing" advertising and to scale up spending with your "winners."

Advertising on the Internet generally falls under one of the three main models:

1. *Cost per impression* (CPM). The *M* is for the Roman numeral denoting "1,000," and thus this is measured as a cost per 1,000 impressions. An impression is when a potential prospect views your advertising, such as a banner advertisement on a web site. Your advertising medium could be a static banner ad, a "media" banner, a pop-up ad (we all hate those, but they're still effective!), solo e-mails sent to a list, a classified ad in an online newsletter, and so on.

2. *Cost per action* (CPA). This is where you pay for some kind of action taken by the prospect, such as the submission of a registration form. Your advertisement might, for instance, offer prospects a free "white paper" or "sample." You would not incur any costs unless/until the prospect filled out and submitted an online registration form supplying his or her contact information. In essence, you're purchasing a real-time lead, and you would generally have a system in place to respond immediately to a prospect's inquiry.

3. *Cost per click* (CPC). With this model, you are paying only when someone clicks on your ad. It might be a text ad, banner, or even video advertisement. This model of advertising is most often associated with the

pay-per-click search engines such as Yahoo! Search Marketing and Google AdWords.

CPM NETWORKS

Each of these companies has contracted with hundreds or thousands of web sites to provide them advertising revenue. For example, I recently went to CNN.com and clicked on an advertisement there—my browser was redirected through the doubleclick.net ad server to the advertiser's landing page.

For each of these companies, you can sign up for an advertising account and submit your advertising creative (text ads, banner ads, and so on), and they manage the placement and rotation of those advertisements on their network sites. You pay for the number of times your text/banner ad is displayed.

http://bannerCAST.com/
http://www.adbrite.com/
http://adsational.com/
http://www.bluelithium.com/
http://www.mammamediasolutions.com/publishers/
   graphic/index.html
http://www.tribalfusion.com/
http://flatfeespectrum.com/
http://www.burstmedia.com/release/advertisers/advertiser.asp
http://www.doubleclick.net/
http://www.theadstop.com/
http://www.hyperbidder.com/

http://www.pradnetwork.com/
http://www.onresponse.com/
http://www.valueclickmedia.com/
http://www.adjungle.com/

CPA NETWORKS

Rather than contracting with web sites, per se, these companies recruit affiliates (see "Affiliate Marketing") to promote performance-based offers. These promotions are frequently done via e-mail. The affiliates (and the company) get paid only when the prospect completes some specified action such as submitting a registration form or downloading some software. As the advertiser, you would set the specific action that must be taken by the prospect.

The less intrusive the action, the less you would pay. For instance, some advertisers will pay whenever someone submits a simple form that asks only for the prospect's zip code. Because there is little resistance to submitting this kind of information, the leads thus generated aren't as valuable as leads that include an e-mail address or phone number.

However, you may find that the submission of a zip code is enough to engage prospects in your sales process and entice them to make a bigger commitment through the submission of their contact information.

As the advertiser, you can specify whether or not your offer can be *incentivized*—which refers to the practice of the promoter giving some kind of bonus to anyone who completes the prescribed action. It generally yields a higher number of lower-cost, less-valuable leads.

    http://leadermarkets.com/
    http://modernclick.com/
    http://www.websponsors.com/
    http://www.4fc.us/
    http://www.cpaempire.com/
    http://www.cpase.com/
    http://www.hydramedia.com/
    http://www.focalex.com/
    http://www.neverblueads.com/
    http://www.offerweb.com/
    http://www.primaryads.com/
    http://www.primeq.com/
    https://www.affiliatefuel.com/advertisers/pricing.html

CPC ADVERTISING

With CPC (also known as *pay per click,* or PPC), you list the keywords related to your product or service and specify how much you're willing to pay for each visit to your site. In some cases, you can also specify the specific sites and pages you want the ads to run on (or *not* to run on).

Your advertisements are then displayed on sites that are determined to be related to your keywords (and/or the sites you specified), and you incur an advertising cost only when and if someone clicks on one of your advertisements. Costs are determined largely by supply and demand—the more popular the keyword that generated the click, the more you will pay for the visit.

While there are literally hundreds of pay-per-click search engines, you should focus on the main three to begin with:

1. Yahoo! Search Marketing
   http://sem.smallbusiness.yahoo.com/searchengine
   marketing/
2. Google Adwords
   http://adwords.google.com/
3. Microsoft Ad Center
   http://advertising.msn.com/microsoft-adcenter

Successful PPC advertising is a topic unto itself—entire books have been written to explain its strategies and nuances. Be sure to read the section on "PPC Advertising" for more resources related to this method of advertising.

CONTEXTUAL ADVERTISING

Contextual advertising is a term that could apply to CPC/PPC advertising. But here I'm talking about advertising triggered by software on the user's computer. This method of advertising has a troubled past and is still somewhat controversial.

There's an ethical (and legal, in most cases) problem if the user doesn't know the software is going to trigger ads. In the past, this function was not disclosed or was hidden in the legalese of the "End User's License Agreement." In addition, there were some shady operators who made the software well-nigh impossible to remove from the user's system. These applications were known as *adware*.

However, as long as the software in question is installed with the full understanding and permission of the user, I believe the ethical requirements have been satisfied.

The way it works is very similar to the PPC search engines from the advertiser's perspective. You simply list the keywords that should trigger the advertisement *or* you list the web site URLs you want to trigger your ads. Contextual advertising can be purchased on a CPM or CPC basis (and even CPA, in some cases).

Then, when users (those who have the contextual advertising software installed on their system) enter a search term in their favorite search engine, and that search term matches your keyword(s), they see your advertisement.

And here is where this form of advertising departs sharply from the PPC model. . . .

The web sites in question have *not* contracted with the contextual advertising company. They have no "space" on their site for the advertisement to appear. The advertisement appears in a new window on top of (or below, if you wish) the web site displayed in the user's browser.

This can be a half-page or even a full-page ad, not a dinky little advertisement in the margins of the web page.

You see why this can be a very controversial form of advertising. Imagine if Ford Motor Company set up a campaign to display its advertisements whenever the user went to the Chevy web site or did a Google search for "Chevrolet truck buy."

As you can see, this form of advertising is both powerful and dangerous—care should be taken when using it.

Here are a few companies with an installed user base allowing them to offer contextual advertising:

http://mediatraffic.com/index.php
http://www.admedian.com/
http://www.zango.com/
http://www.whenu.com/
http://www.adonnetwork.com/
http://www.clicksor.com/
http://www.memedia.com/
https://www.mycustomersdirect.com/

E-MAIL ADVERTISING

Despite the ever-increasing volume of spam consumers must deal with, e-mail advertising can still be highly effective.

Remember, the proper function of advertising is to get people to "raise their hand" (i.e., demonstrate their interest in your product). Don't try to sell something in an e-mail to a list not already acquainted with you—your offer should be for a free report, a sample, or something similar.

These companies allow you to place advertisements in existing e-mail publications or send out solo e-mails to various e-mail lists. Note that all of these lists will have been built using accepted opt-in methods.

http://www.optininc.com/
http://www.edithroman.com/
http://www.postmasternetwork.net/
http://www.yesmail.com/
http://www.ientry.com/page/ad/
http://www.ezines-r-us.com/targeted-solo-ads/
http://www.demc.com/
http://www.directoryofezines.com/
http://www.ezinead.net/
http://ezineadvertising.com/
http://www.list-city.com/advertise.shtml
http://www.ideamarketers.com/publish/psearch.cfm
http://www.topezineads.com/
http://www.list-city.com/advertise.shtml
http://www.ezinead.net/

RSS ADVERTISING

These companies place your ads between news items in RSS readers (see "RSS").

http://www.feedburner.com/fb/a/advertising
http://www.bidvertiser.com/
http://www.pheedo.com/site/adv_overview.php

MISCELLANEOUS ADVERTISING RESOURCES

Yes, some of these are for advertisements that run external to the Internet—but if you use these to drive people to your web site, I still call it "Internet marketing" . . . and these resources *are* online.

NEWPAPER ADVERTISING

For discount newspaper advertising (specializing in remnant space in newspapers), try this site:

http://www.mss-standby.com/

Newspaper classified advertising networks allow you to place your classified ad in several newspapers with a single ad-insertion order. For instance, one of the current offers is to place your 20-word classified ad in 20 newspapers with a total circulation of 1 million people for $180.

Another offer is for a total circulation of 14 million people for $1,400, which represents a cost per thousand (CPM) of just 10 cents! (For comparison, you'll usually pay a CPM of anywhere from $2.00 to $20.00 or more for banner or e-mail advertising.)

Now, these *are* classified ads we're talking about, so that CPM comparison isn't exactly apples to apples . . . but even if only 1 in 10,000 people looks at your classified ad, you're still talking about a low CPM cost of $1.00.

Another consideration is the kind of papers being advertised in. Many of these are small-town weekly newspapers and *PennySaver* or *Thrifty Nickel* types of papers, so they have a longer usable life than a daily newspaper.

The real value in these services is that you place only *one* order to get your advertisement in as many as 700 different publications—a huge time saver!

http://www.nationwideadvertising.com/
http://www.budget-ads.com/

This company offers to place your advertisement in *USA Today* at a discounted rate:

http://www.wolfenterprises.net/usatoday.html

Radio Advertising

http://www.bid4spots.com/
http://www.swmxradio.com/
http://satellite-radio-advertising.com/

TV Advertising

http://www.cheap-tv-spots.com/

Online Video Advertising

http://www.jivox.com/
https://adwords.google.com/select/videoads.html

Print Advertising Bids

http://www.mediabids.com/

Advertising Creativity Tools

http://www.adcracker.com/

Advertising Games

http://www.advergame.com/

Advertising Text Ads

http://www.adster.com/
http://www.Text-Link-Ads.com/

Online Classified Ad Sites

http://www.craigslist.com/
http://base.google.com/
http://www.usfreeads.com/
http://www.kijiji.com/

(In addition, eBay offers classified ads in a few specific categories—see more about that under "eBay.")

Per-Inquiry Advertising

http://www.hpowermarketing.com/

Affiliate Marketing

This concept has been around since Amazon first implemented an affiliate program on its site, yet many people still don't know what an affiliate program is.

An affiliate promotes a product on behalf of a merchant. For instance, if you sign up at Amazon.com as an affiliate, you can then add special links on your web site (or in your e-mails) to direct people to the listing for specific books at Amazon.com. If somebody goes to Amazon.com via your affiliate link and purchases the featured product, you get a commission from Amazon.

Affiliates can be paid based on any combination of CPM, CPC, CPA, or CPS. We've discussed the first three—ad impressions, visits, and actions. In *cost per sale* (CPS), the affiliate is paid only when a sale is made.

Being paid based on advertising views (CPM) is rare, unless the affiliate is an advertising network. Being paid based on clicks is usually reserved for affiliates of PPC search engines.

For most merchants, affiliates will be paid based on leads generated (CPA) or sales. This is great for the merchants because they are paying only for performance. If the affiliate's efforts generate no leads or sales, it costs the merchant nothing.

Of course, this is a double-edged sword. If the merchant's sales copy can't convert enough of the affiliate's visitors, the affiliate will not make any money and will then start promoting a different merchant's product! So it really is a case of "you scratch my back and I'll scratch yours."

Because of this, it would be wise for you to make sure you have a proven sales process in place before implementing any kind of affiliate program. Once you know you'll convert X percent of your site visitors, you can give affiliates a reasonable estimate of the revenue they can expect their traffic to yield.

A merchant can implement an affiliate program in three different ways, and they all have their advantages and disadvantages.

1. *Use one of the affiliate networks.* You sign up as a merchant, and the affiliate network recruits affiliates who can then choose to promote your product or service. You pay the affiliate network for the actions or sales generated by their affiliates, and the network pays the affiliates responsible for generating them.

   Advantages: The network already has thousands of affiliates, so you don't need to spend a lot of time recruiting new ones. The network also takes care of all the affiliate payments and end-of-year tax paperwork (e.g., 1099 forms in the United States).

The network handles the affiliate inquiries regarding how to set up its links, payment schedules, and so forth.

Disadvantages: You don't get the same level of communications access to the affiliates—in some cases you don't even know who they are. They're not *your* affiliates; they belong to the network. If you leave the network, you can't take the affiliates with you. Costs can be prohibitive for small and/or start-up businesses.

2. *Use hosted affiliate program software.* You pay a monthly or yearly fee for use of the affiliate program software. This software tracks all visits, actions, and sales generated by the affiliates and automatically credits affiliates for them.

   Advantages: Any affiliates who come into your program are *your* affiliates. You have unlimited communications access to them, and if you opt to go with a different affiliate solution, you can take your affiliates with you.

   Disadvantages: You start out with zero affiliates and must recruit them yourself. You are also responsible for affiliate payments and tax filing. You will have a higher level of support requirements for your affiliates (they will be sending their inquiries to *you* rather than to an affiliate network).

3. *Use your affiliate software installed on your own web server.* You pay a one-time fee for software to be installed on your own web server (in some cases, there is an

additional monthly or yearly support/maintenance fee). In many cases, this software also serves as your cart/e-commerce system, and the affiliate functions are an integral part of the order process. Usually, the software can be customized to your specific requirements.

Advantages: You have complete control over every aspect of your affiliate program. Affiliates you recruit are yours and can be imported to another solution should you choose to do so. You are not dependant on a third-party server being "up" for your affiliates to be credited for the actions or sales they generate. Over the long term, this is generally the least expensive solution.

Disadvantages: You must recruit your own affiliates and provide support for them. You are responsible for all affiliate payments and tax filing. The standard features of the affiliate system may not be as cutting edge as those offered by a hosted solution (although you can overcome this with customization).

A growing number of people make a full-time income as affiliates—promoting other people's products and not dealing with any of the headaches normally associated with business (customer support, manufacturing problems, distribution issues, etc.).

Even if it's not your exclusive income source, it can be an easy-to-implement secondary revenue stream.

AFFILIATE NETWORKS

These companies implement tracking mechanisms whereby merchants may offer and affiliates may promote various products and services. Affiliates may be paid on a per-sale, per-click, or per-lead (a.k.a. per-action) basis.

http://www.cj.com/
http://www.maxbounty.com/
http://www.websponsors.com/
http://www.filinet.com/
http://www.affiliatenetwork.com/
http://www.linkshare.com/
http://www.clickbank.com/
http://www.shareasale.com/
http://chitika.com/
http://www.paydotcom.com

MERCHANT RESOURCES

If you want to implement your own affiliate program and pay affiliates for promoting your products, consider these resources. See also "Affiliate Networks."

Affiliate Acquisition

These tools help you identify potential affiliates to promote your product:

http://www.affiliateelite.com/
http://scamfreezone.com/spider/

http://www.linkcapture.com/
http://www.axandra-link-popularity-tool.com/index.htm
http://pjltechnology.com/affiliatelocator.htm

Here's a web site that lists several available affiliate management courses and certification programs. It also lists some companies that will do the affiliate management for you:

http://www.affiliateguide.com/affiliate-management.html

Affiliate Program Software

(Note that most of today's integrated e-commerce solutions also include affiliate functions. See "E-Commerce Integrated Systems" for more information.)

These are hosted on the *provider's* server:

http://www.assoctrac.com/
http://www.directtrack.com/

These are installed on *your* server:

http://www.affiliatesoftware.net/
http://www.interneka.com/
http://www.groundbreak.com/
http://dhsoftwares.com/
http://www.qualityunit.com/
http://www.myaffiliateprogram.com/

http://www.affiliateshop.com/
http://jrox.com/
http://www.jvmanager.com/index.shtml
http://www.postaffiliatepro.com/
http://www.idevdirect.com/

Affiliate Program Promotion

These are places where you can announce your new affiliate program:

http://www.affiliateannouncement.com/
http://www.affiliatefirst.com/submit/

AFFILIATE RESOURCES

If you want to sell third-party products or services as an affiliate, these resources may be helpful. For promoting digitally delivered products as an affiliate, see also "ClickBank."

Affiliate Commission Collections. Sad but true, some merchants will fail to pay their affiliates for the sales they've generated. This company works with the affiliates to collect the commissions they are due:
http://www.affiliatecollectionagency.com/

Affiliate Organizer. If you're involved with many affiliate programs, it can be a nightmare keeping track of all the accounts and campaigns. This company offers a software management solution to help you keep things organized:
http://www.affiliateorganizer.com/

Affiliate Program Directories

If you are looking for products that appeal to your site visitors (without directly competing with your own products and services), check out these affiliate directories.

They'll tell you exactly what is available to promote as an affiliate and what the commissions are. Some of these will also give you the conversion rates the offers are currently generating (so you don't spend your time promoting a losing offer).

Naturally, if you have a product you want affiliates to promote, these directories would be a good place for you to be listed:

http://www.associateprograms.com/
http://www.affiliatefirst.com/
http://www.refer-it.com/
http://www.2-tier.com/
http://www.affiliatesdirectory.com/
http://www.netshops.com/

In addition, all of the companies listed in "Affiliate Networks" list the various products that can be promoted by their affiliates.

Affiliate Training

The competition among affiliates is fierce, so I've made an exception to my "no training courses" rule in this case. On these sites you can find some of the more effective affiliate training courses. If you're serious about affiliate marketing, you should invest in at least one of these:

http://www.netprofitstoday.com/
http://www.thesecondtier.com/
http://www.secretaffiliateweapon.com/
http://www.work-at-home-net-guides.com/

Other Resources

These web server programs will build entire stores on your site based on an affiliate merchant's data feed:

http://www.c3scripts.com/index.html
http://www.pricetapestry.com/
http://datafeedstudio.com/
http://www.mydatafeedscripts.com/
http://www.finditfastgold.com/

This site offers an affiliate ROI analysis service:

http://www.nichetracker.com/

For affiliate programs domain forwarding, check out:

http://namestick.com/

Article
Marketing

Article marketing is a very simple concept. You write articles and post them to the various article directories. Each article contains a "resource box" at the bottom where you include your contact information.

If you're smart, you'll include more than just a web site address in your resource box—you'll give people a tantalizing reason for visiting your site (or opting in to your publication). There are a couple of effective techniques for doing this.

One idea is to make your articles part of a series (e.g., offer Part 1, Part 2, etc.). Then, at the bottom of each article, you'd have a link to "Visit example.com to read Part 2, '10 Secret Sources for Cheap Widgets,'" or something along those lines.

Another idea is to offer a free white paper or some such report in your resource box. You can have people visit your web site to get the report, or you can have them send a blank e-mail to an autoresponder e-mail address and send the report to them that way. (We discuss autoresponders later in this book.)

There has been some debate recently concerning the effectiveness of article marketing. If done right, I believe it can still be extremely effective. Not only do you get the direct result of people visiting your site from the article, but in cases where the article directory allows your resource box to contain a live link, you also get a better reputation from the search engines.

One drawback to article marketing is that it can be rather time-intensive. You must submit your article to each article directory. Fortunately, several software packages are available to take the drudgery out of the whole thing by submitting articles for you. Here are three:

http://www.articleequalizer.com/
http://www.articleannouncer.com/
http://www.interlogy.com/products/content/article/

Or, if you just want to let someone else do the whole thing, use an article distribution service:

http://www.articledashboard.com/
http://thephantomwriters.com/x.pl/tpw/index.html

The other problem with article marketing is that you must—guess what?—actually *write* the articles! For article marketing to be effective, you want as many articles out there as possible—over time, hundreds or even thousands. A good start would be 10 articles a week.

If you don't have time for writing all those articles, consider having others do it for you (see "Outsourcing").

Audio

Web audio has been practically eclipsed by video, but there are still times when it makes sense to add an audio file to your site. Common uses include recorded testimonials or an audio sales or thank-you message.

Audio can be added using software on your own computer or through a subscription service. The services are best when you need something right now, but you'll save money and have more control in the long run by getting your own software. (If you use a service, be sure to keep a local backup of all your audio messages.)

AUDIO EDITING

http://audacity.sourceforge.net/

AUDIO CONTENT PROVIDERS

http://www.findsounds.com/
http://www.smartsound.com/
http://www.digitaljuice.com/

SERVICES FOR ADDING AUDIO TO YOUR SITE

http://www.audiogenerator.com/
http://www.instantaudio.com/
http://www.iprotalk.com/

SOFTWARE FOR ADDING AUDIO TO YOUR SITE

http://www.totalwebaudio.com/
http://www.audioacrobat.com/
http://www.mp3streamingaudio.com/
http://www.audiomakerpro.com/
http://www.theaudiokit.com/
http://www.acoustica.com/

AUDIO FILE CONVERSION

These allow you to convert from one audio format to another:

http://www.coolutils.com/TotalAudioConverter/
http://zamzar.com/
http://www.erightsoft.com/SUPER.html/

AUDIO EQUIPMENT

http://www.soundprofessionals.com/
http://www.internetaudioguy.com/

AUDIO TRANSCRIPT SERVICE

http://www.escriptionist.com/
http://www.enablr.com/

(see also "Transcription Services")

AUDIO VOICE-OVER SERVICE

http://www.easyivr.com/provoice.htm
http://www.amazingvoice.com/
http://voice123.com/

Autoresponder Services/ Software

Autoresponders have been available for at least a dozen years now, but a surprising number of people have never heard of them. In it's simplest form, an autoresponder is a program that automatically responds to an e-mail inquiry.

You send an e-mail to a specific e-mail address, and a preprogrammed response is immediately sent to your e-mail. Originally, it was all done via e-mail, but now it can be done via online forms you fill out and submit.

While simple autoresponders can still be useful for some things (and are included in most web hosting packages), they have been largely supplanted by *sequential autoresponders*.

With a sequential autoresponder, you still get the immediate response, but the system can also be set up to send you additional information at regularly scheduled intervals. So you might receive the initial response followed by another e-mail two days later . . . and another one a week after that. Most services allow an unlimited number of follow-up messages.

Marketing experts are all in agreement that a well-crafted follow-up sequence of e-mails (most recommend a minimum of seven) will boost your overall sales conversion significantly—a 100 percent improvement in conversion is not even considered extraordinary.

Most sequential autoresponder services allow the merchant to send out e-mail broadcasts to anyone who is in the system—so they can now be used for mail list management as well.

In addition to the various services, you can install software on your web server that functions in the same way. However, given the hostile environment your e-mails must navigate, I recommend using a well-established service in lieu of your own software—the deliverability will be higher over the long run, *and* there will be less risk of choking the server if and when you develop a large mailing list.

One of the few personal recommendations I make in this guide is for the AWeber service. That's not to say the others aren't good, but I have personally used AWeber for several years and it has been rock-solid.

See also under "E-Mail Marketing."

Autoresponder Hosted Services

http://www.aweber.com/
http://www.emaillabs.com/
http://www.getresponse.com/
http://www.quicktell.com/indexa.htm
http://www.emailaces.com/
http://www.proautoresponder.com

Autoresponder Software

http://www.autoresponseplus.com/
http://www.listmailpro.com/

This software tool helps you to quickly create the messages for your follow-up sequence. It's not totally automated, but will certainly save you a good deal of time:

http://www.instantnicheemails.com/

Backup

Sooner or later you're going to have a computer crash, a fire, a flood, or maybe just a really nasty computer virus. Do you make regular backups of your important files? If you do, pat yourself on the back—you're doing better than most.

However, to be really safe you need to have off-site backups. That way, if your whole office is taken out, your valuable data can still be retrieved.

These services give you an online storage area to back up your computer data so that it's geographically isolated from your location. (See also "File Hosting.")

https://www.idrive.com/
http://www.altexa.com/
http://www.thebackupsite.com/
http://mozy.com/
http://www.sync2s3.com/
http://www.ibackup.com/
http://www.xdrive.com/

Not only should you back up your local data to an off-site location, but your web site should be backed up, too. Most web hosting companies offer backup services, and some of them even offer off-site backup. But just to be safe, you should have a local copy of your web site files. This software does just that:

http://www.cpsitesaver.com/(for cPanel hosting accounts)
http://www.site-vault.com/
http://remote-backup.com/siteshelter/

Blogs

Okay, I admit it—blogs are just not my thing. I have one (anyone who is anyone has one, right?), but I've sorely neglected my readers . . . mostly because I've been working on this book, which is a lame excuse. But still.

Word has it, though, that blogs are glorious creatures to behold. And *when* the writer regularly publishes, blogs are all the rage in the search-engine-placement world. Search engines love blogs, indexing them within just a few minutes in many cases. Everyone should have one and should use it. (Do as I say, not as I do!)

In fact, it's not a bad idea to have multiple blogs. You should have one on each of your web sites.

For effective product launches (see www.productlaunch formula.com), blogs are an essential part of the communications feedback loop between you and your prospects and customers, and may even warrant a separate "launch updates" blog in addition to your main site blog.

BLOG SOFTWARE

For setting up a blog on your server, the two most popular open-source (free) solutions are:

http://wordpress.org/
http://movabletype.org/

I use WordPress and it seems to be the more popular of the two options (at least in Internet marketing circles). Some people have suggested that Movable Type is the better choice if you want to run multiple blogs from a central admin panel.

In addition to these blog solutions, most content management systems (see "Content Management") can be set up with a blog, in addition to many other functions.

BLOG SERVICES

In addition to having a blog on your own server, you can set up blogs on hosted services in just a few minutes. These are very popular with the search engines, so you can get some extra play with them—just make sure you're not posting the exact same thing on multiple blogs. That's a no-no! Here are the most popular hosted blog services:

http://www.blogger.com/
http://wordpress.com/signup/
http://www.bloglines.com/
http://www.blogspot.com/
http://www.typepad.com/

BLOG PINGING SERVICES

Whenever you create a new blog post (and assuming you want people to know it's there), you will want to notify the blog aggregator services—this is referred to as sending them a *ping*. This tells everyone to come check out your latest post.

Depending on the software you have, this may be done automatically. For instance, WordPress defaults to sending a ping to Ping-O-Matic with each post. If not, here are a couple of services that send to multiple aggregators:

http://www.pingoat.com/
http://pingomatic.com/

BLOG DIRECTORIES AND SEARCH ENGINES

http://www.getblogs.com/
http://www.technorati.com/
http://www.bloglines.com/

Also check out AWeber's "blog to e-mail" feature—you can set your blog so that whenever you publish new material, that content goes out to an e-mail list. Pretty nifty.

CGI Scripts

When I talk about "CGI scripts," I'm talking about software that is installed on your web server and is usually used in some kind of interaction with your visitors. This might be form-processing software to handle your "contact form," shopping cart or order-processing software, affiliate software, or an infinite number of other possibilities. Sometimes it interacts only with you, the site administrator (e.g., traffic analysis tools).

The most popular programming languages for Unix/Linux web servers are PHP and Perl. If your web site is hosted on a Windows server, the programs will most likely be done with "Active Server Pages" (ASP).

(Usually PHP software doesn't use the Common Gateway Interface (CGI) and therefore is not technically CGI software—but the result is the same for the users. They fill out a form, click a button, and see some kind of results based on their input.)

There's no way I could link to every useful server-based software program available to you—but here are several sites where you can poke around and see what they've got to offer. If you have a specific need, you can usually find something that fits. Sometimes just browsing the software descriptions will give you ideas you hadn't thought of before.

CGI SCRIPT SITES

http://www.sitegadgets.com/
http://scriptsearch.internet.com/
http://www.worldwidecreations.com/
http://worldwidecreations.com/freescripts.htm
http://www.jansfreeware.com/
http://www.perlcoders.com/
http://www.perlmasters.com/
http://www.rlaj.com/scripts/
http://www.c3scripts.com/index.html
http://willmaster.com/master/
http://www.worldwidecreations.com/webmasterscriptkit.htm
http://www.BontragerCGI.com/
http://www.bignosebird.com/cgi.shtml
http://cgi.resourceindex.com/
http://www.extropia.com/applications.html
http://www.hotscripts.com/
http://www.mrcgiguy.com/
http://www.cgiconnection.com/

CGI SCRIPT INSTALLATION

Once you purchase the software, you need to install it on
your web server (unless installation is included with your purchase). Usually it's a straightforward process—but if you
don't want to tackle it yourself, here are a few resources that
do that kind of thing. Some of these will also customize
scripts for you.

http://www.cgihub.com/
http://www.webfresh.com/
http://www.applytools.com/install.html
http://www.islandseven.com/cgi/
http://cgi.resourceindex.com/Programmers/
http://scriptinstallation.com/

You can also get help with script installation from the various outsourcing resources listed later in this book (see "Outsourcing").

Chat Services

A chat room allows you to communicate in real time (via keyboard) with several people at once. This can be a great way to build your community—for example, by having a "Weekly Wednesday Chat" every Wednesday at 2:00 P.M. Or perhaps your customers would enjoy an informal Q&A session just before you launch a new product.

It doesn't make sense when you have only one or two people to talk with (just pick up the phone or use Skype for that), but if you have 10 to 20 people all yammering at once, an online chat makes a lot more sense.

Several web hosting accounts include chat functions, but they're generally not very good. These services offer good performance at low cost:

http://www.parachat.com/
http://www.talkcity.com/

See also "Communications," as some of those sites may offer conferencing capabilities.

ClickBank

ClickBank is such a popular affiliate network that it gets its own section. ClickBank is popular because it's easy for the merchant to set up and easy for the affiliate to promote. Here's how it works:

Anyone can sign up for a ClickBank account free of charge. When you initially sign up, you are an affiliate. You can go to the ClickBank "Marketplace" and browse the various categories to see what's being sold. You can also see what the commission rate is for various "products," and how well they are selling.

Once you find something you want to promote, just grab the copy-and-paste code and add that to your site to create the product link. If someone clicks on the link and buys the product, you get a commission. ClickBank pays every two weeks and has a sterling reputation for prompt payment.

Now, if you want to *sell* products, the process is pretty simple. You set up your product sales and thank-you pages and enter some information in your account "product" screen. Then wait for ClickBank's approval (which usually comes back the same day).

ClickBank charges a one-time fee of $49.95 for the privilege of selling through its system, and for each sale it charges you $1.00 plus 7.5 percent, which may seem somewhat on the high side when you compare it to the 2 to 3 percent cost of processing credit cards with your own merchant account, but remember that the fee includes managing the affiliate payments, taxes, support, and so on. It's a great way for someone on a shoestring budget to start out.

Caveat: ClickBank requires that you sell a digitally delivered product. That means e-books, software, online memberships, and so on—anything that can be delivered via the Internet instead of a tangible, physically delivered product.

Oh, and speaking of memberships, ClickBank does include the ability to have products with recurring billing—so if you want to, you can charge $20 per month for access to your "members-only" area.

Some of these tools are designed for ClickBank affiliates, some for ClickBank merchants, and some will help both.

CLICKBANK HELP

http://www.ClickBankGuide.com/

CLICKBANK MANAGEMENT SOFTWARE

http://cbextract.com/
http://www.easyclickmate.com/

CLICKBANK ADS SERVICE

http://www.cbprosense.net/
http://clicksensor.com/

CLICKBANK ADS SOFTWARE

http://www.cbplugin.com/
http://www.cbmaximizer.com/
http://www.cbnichebuilder.com/
http://www.affiliatesensor.com/
http://www.cbcontext.com/
http://www.clickbank-ads.com/

CLICKBANK MALL

http://www.CBmall.com/
http://1stpromotion.com/

CLICKBANK TOOLS

http://www.clickbankaccountant.com/
http://www.affiliatesalert.com/

Communications

When you're talking about online business tools, they're *all* about communications in one way or another. But here we're talking about communicating one-on-one with your customers or prospects.

Some of these resources offer multiple services. For instance, some of the fax services also offer voice-mail options.

LIVE OPERATOR

When people are looking at your online sales presentation and want to ask a question, they can click the "Got a Question? Ask Our Live Operator!" button to be connected with a real person in a text chat window. There are a lot of web services and software packages that will implement this kind of functionality.

Several also allow you to monitor visitors (i.e., to see which pages they're looking at and how long they've been there) and push a message out to them. It's the online shopping version of the floor salesperson coming up to you and asking, "Is there anything in particular I can help you find today?"

This can actually backfire if done incorrectly (some people get a little freaked out!). But if done right, it can have a huge impact on the profitability of your site.

Not only will you close more sales, but you will gather extremely valuable feedback from your site visitors. For instance, if you see a pattern of people asking whether you have a guarantee, that is a good clue that you need to emphasize your guarantee more on your sales page.

Ari Galper trains people and companies in the proper use of this technology, and I highly recommend his services:

http://www.chatwise.com/

HOSTED SERVICES

Here are some live-operator services, some of which also have click-to-call services integrated into their text chat functions:

http://www.websitealive.com/
http://www.livehelper.com/
http://www.liveperson.com/
http://www.groopz.com/
http://phplivesupport.com/
http://www.estara.com/
http://www.upsellit.com/
http://www.liveassistance.com/
http://www.InstantService.com/
http://www.meebome.com/

SERVER SOFTWARE

You can also install software on your web server to function in the same way. Here are a few of the available packages:

http://worldwidecreations.com/active_stats.htm
http://phpopenchat.org/

http://phplivesupport.com/
http://www.liveservicedesk.com/
http://www.craftysyntax.com/ (free)
http://www.siteinteractive.com/liveadvisor/

CLICK-TO-CALL

This is the next level of contact with your customers. They can click on a click-to-call button on your web site and be connected to your operator for a live phone conversation. Some companies have reported a doubling of their web site conversion rates using this technology.

Here are some of the companies that offer click-to-call services:

http://www.estara.com/estara/
http://www.netcallplc.com/
http://www.zifftalk.com/
http://public.ifbyphone.com/
http://www.clicktocall.com/

FAX BROADCASTING

Fax broadcasting allows you to upload a list of your fax contacts and have your fax letter sent to all of them. Fax broadcasting is an extremely efficient and inexpensive way to get time-sensitive information to your clients.

Just make sure you have their written permission, and make sure to check your local laws first—this form of marketing is legal only when certain conditions have been met. Again, check your local laws.

Here are some fax broadcasting services:

http://www.FlatRateFax.com/
http://www.broadfax.com/
http://www.jblast.com/
http://www.faxbroadcasters.com/

FAX AND VOICE-MAIL SERVICES

These services allow you to receive your faxes and voice mail online. When a fax transmission or voice mail comes in, you get an e-mail notification, and you can read the fax or listen to your voice mail right online:

http://www.j2.com/
http://www.ureach.com/
http://www.patlive.com/
http://www.efax.com/
http://www.faxaway.com/

INSTANT MESSAGING SOFTWARE

This software allows you to send instant messages to people (who also must have an instant messaging program running) at their computers or mobile phones.

You can add people to your list of contacts, which makes it possible for them to see when you're online and thus able to receive messages.

http://www.icq.com/
http://www.aim.com/
http://messenger.yahoo.com/
http://messenger.msn.com/

Also see "Miscellaneous Resources," under "Voice over IP," since most VoIP services have this capability as well.

UNIVERSAL INSTANT MESSENGERS

These universal instant messenger applications allow you to use in a single application the instant messaging from several services simultaneously.

http://www.trillian.cc/
http://www.pidgin.im/
http://www.meebo.com/

VIRTUAL PHONE SYSTEM

Advertised as having "all the features of an expensive PBX, for about the same price you're currently paying for voicemail."

http://www.pbnext.com/

TOLL-FREE NUMBERS

http://kall8.com/rates.htm
http://www.tollfreenumbers.com/
http://www.get800today.com/

CENTRALIZED PHONE SERVICES

These allow you to give out one phone number for multiple phones, fax, and so on.

http://www.grandcentral.com/
http://www.linxcom.com/

VOICE-TO-TEXT

This is something I personally use and *love*. When someone calls me and leaves a message on my voice mail, the voice-to-text service instantly translates the voice message to text (using a computer text-to-speech program) and e-mails that message to me.

Its accuracy is simply amazing—it even correctly transcribed "supercalifragilisticexpialidocious" (I tested it)!

In cases where the text isn't clear, you can listen to the voice message—it's sent as an attachment to the e-mail. The service I use is PhoneTag.com, and the others offer similar features.

http://www.phonetag.com/
http://www.spinvox.com/
http://www.phonewire.com/cc/
http://www.callwave.com/

Conferencing

When you want to get a large number of people (25 to 2,000) on a phone call, most office systems won't have the capacity you require, so use these services for your teleseminars and webinars.

Some of these services include recording/transcription features, and some will even allow you to see who exactly is on the call. See also "Voice over IP" (under "Miscellaneous Resources").

Even though the call is normally recorded, sooner or later something will go wrong—so you should hedge your bets by also recording the call yourself.

http://eagleconf.com/
http://www.allconferencing.com/
http://www.accuconference.com/
http://www.freeconferencecall.com/
http://www.btconferencing.com/btc/index.asp
http://www.rentabridge.com/
http://www.freeconference.com/WebScheduled800.asp
http://www.voicetext.com/
http://24conference.com/
http://www.voxwire.com/

http://iconcommunicator.com/33656/
http://freeconferencing.liveoffice.com/

With webinars, your prospects can watch a screencast while listening to you on the phone. On their computer, they see whatever you are broadcasting from yours.

http://www.webinars.com/
http://www.gotowebinar.com/
http://www.webex.com/smb/webinars.html
https://www.megameeting.com/

More information about how to promote your business using webinars can be found here:

http://www.WebinarSecrets.com

Content Management

If you just have a 3- to 10-page static "mini site," you don't really need a content management system—FTP will work just fine.

If you "don't do" FTP and have a fairly simple web site design in mind, you may be able to use standard blog software as your content management system—see "Blogs" for some suggested software.

However, if you have a *lot* of content and want to automate the scheduling and publishing of new content, then a good content management system is required.

A content management system will allow you to make sitewide changes quickly and will give you the power to easily integrate dynamic data. Browse these sites and you'll be amazed by the possibilities.

Here are some of the most popular content management systems:

http://www.joomla.org/
http://www.drupal.org/
http://www.typo3.com/

http://modxcms.com/
http://www.tikiwiki.org/
http://www.typolight.org/
http://plone.org/
http://mamboserver.com/
http://www.mstay.com/index.html
http://www.siteworkspro.com/
http://www.postnuke.com/
http://www.xoops.org/

Content Suppliers

If you want people to come back to your site and stick around for a bit while they're there, you must have high-quality, frequently updated content. There are three main ways of doing this:

1. *Create or commission the creation of original content, exclusive to your site.* There's not much to explain here . . . you write/create the content, or you pay someone else to do it for you.
2. *Have the content created automatically by your community.* By adding some of the tools discussed under "CGI Scripts," you can have much of the content of your site created automatically by your site community. Things like forums, wikis, blogs, video sharing, and so on will constantly add new content with very little effort of your own.
3. *Use third-party content from article and syndication feed sites.* These sites contain literally millions of articles that you can add to your site or newsletter. Most of these have syndication feeds—see "Really Simple

Syndication (RSS)"—or other mechanisms you can use to insert the article(s) of interest on your site by simply adding a tiny snippet of code to the page.

Here are some of the sites that offer such content:

http://www.ideamarketers.com/publishers.cfm
http://www.freesticky.com/
http://www.amazines.com/
http://www.articledashboard.com/
http://www.certificate.net/wwio/
http://www.contentinfusion.com/
http://www.syndic8.com/
http://rssfeedreader.com/
http://www.site-reference.com/syndicate.php
http://www.goarticles.com/
http://www.mochila.com/
http://www.niche-content-packages.com/
http://www.1st-4-articles.com/
http://www.ContentXperts.com/
http://www.ezinearticles.com/
http://www.articlecity.com/
http://www.ezinearticles.com/content/hyperseek.cgi

See also "Graphics" for web graphics, stock photography, cartoons, and so on.

Copywriting

To maximize your online sales, you need hard-hitting copy that pulls your prospects in close, gets them emotionally attached to your product, and gives them just enough logic to justify their emotional decision to buy it.

This is true for every component of your marketing funnel, from the very first exposure (your lead-generating advertisement) through your follow-up sequence, including the sales page, order form, and order confirmation page.

But we're not finished yet. You also need it in all of your after-the-sale communications, right up to and through the next sale, and then you start all over again.

Copywriting isn't just about the written word, either—and this is especially true on the Internet.

Your web page (if it's optimized for conversion) will likely have embedded audio and video components. Everything needs to be designed with the sole purpose of selling the prospect on taking the next step, be it opting in to your newsletter, submitting an application form, or purchasing your product.

So, you either need to have someone in your organization learn the art and science of copywriting or you need to outsource this task . . . perhaps a little of both.

COPYWRITERS

If nobody in your business has the time or inclination to learn good copywriting skills, hiring a professional copywriter is really the only option that makes sense. Here are a few to consider.

I've seen the work of many of these, and I feel good about recommending them for your consideration . . . but you still need to check them out for yourself!

http://www.bly.com/
http://www.directcontactpr.com/
http://www.Red-Hot-Copy.com/
http://www.controlbeaters.com/
http://www.overnight-copy.com/
http://www.mikejezek.com/
http://www.nickusborne.com/
http://www.orangebeetle.com/copywriting.htm
http://www.peterstonecopy.com/
http://www.renegnam.com/
http://www.thewritesolutionllc.com/
http://www.rayedwardscopy.com/

Copywriting Instruction

Want to learn to do copywriting yourself? Because I consider this a valuable skill to have, I have included a few how-to links in this section, and these courses are (as you would expect) very compelling. . . .

http://www.makepeacetotalpackage.com/
http://bencivengabullets.com/2-030504.asp

http://www.rayedwardscopywriting.com/
http://www.thegaryhalbertletter.com/
http://rayedwards.com/
http://www.NextDay-Copy.com/
http://www.amazingformula.com/
http://www.copysurgery.com/
http://www.paulstoolbox.com/powercopywriting/
http://www.sellingtohumannature.com/
http://www.mastersofcopywriting.com/
http://www.UltimateCopywritingWorkshop.com/
http://www.WebCopySecrets.com/

COPYWRITING SWIPE FILES

If you're going to write copy, don't try to reinvent the wheel. Immerse yourself in other successful ads and swipe the *ideas and tactics* (not the copy!) used therein:

http://scriptorium.lib.duke.edu/adaccess/
http://www.ultimate-online-swipe-file.com/
http://www.WebAdMagic.com/
http://www.adflip.com/
http://www.hypnoticwritingswipefile.com/

COPYWRITING SOFTWARE

I know, I know—you're not going to create a 40-year control piece with this software. But if you follow the formula, you should at least get a good rough draft that follows most of the rules. . . . Hey, it's a start!

http://www.pushbuttonletters.com/

LETTER TEMPLATES

For a shortcut in creating your own sales letters and other prospect and customer communications, consider Yanik Silver's fill-in-the-blank templates:

http://www.instantsalesletters.com/

Co-registration

Cooperative registration is a method of getting leads from other people's web traffic. Here's how it works.

Say you were signing up for an online newsletter about gardening supplies. You would go through the subscription form, entering your name, e-mail address, and whatever additional information was requested.

Just above the "Submit" button, there would be a little checkbox, and next to that it would say something like, "Would you like a free subscription to *Greenhouse Goodies*? If so, check this box and you will be automatically subscribed."

If you check the box and then submit the form, you would be subscribed to the gardening newsletter as you had originally planned, but your lead information would also be sent to the company managing the *Greenhouse Goodies* newsletter.

Co-registration leads have an extremely short life span and should be followed up on within *minutes* for best results. If you wait hours or longer, the subscriber will likely forget about his or her impulsive click and may consider your e-mail communications to be unsolicited—prompting allegations of spam marketing against your company.

Because of this, you must be extremely careful when implementing a co-registration campaign. Getting the co-registration service to host your response e-mails and web pages on *its* server will help you to insulate your own company's reputation against errant spam claims.

And speaking of errant spam claims, they can be just as damaging to your operations as legitimate spam claims. Many Internet service providers have policies such that "If the end user calls it spam, it *is* spam"—that is, they shoot first (shut down your server) and ask questions later.

Even if you're conducting your e-mail marketing in a legitimate way, the so-called appearance of evil can result in a nightmare of red tape and downtime.

Because of this, you need to do *more* than adhere to the letter of the law. You should use "confirmed opt-in" and carefully craft your messages such that they are welcomed by the reader as "requested" communications. Mail regularly enough that people will remember who you are, and always remind them why they are receiving your e-mails (i.e., *how* they got on your list).

Here are some companies that manage co-registration campaigns:

http://www.coregmedia.com/
http://www.permissiondirect.com/
http://www.incentaclick.com/coregistration.php
http://opt-intelligence.com/
http://www.yesmail.com/
http://www.advertisingknowhow.com/

Credibility/Trust

Several conversion authorities have tested the difference in their conversion rate when they have the "Hacker Safe," "TRUSTe," and similar logos on their site.

You'll have to test this yourself, of course, to see how much difference it makes in *your* business—a study several years ago showed that drawing attention to the order page being secure actually brought up concerns about security that the visitors wouldn't otherwise have had.

You can also get logos from your payment processing gateway (AuthorizeNet, PayPal, etc.), shipping company (FedEx, even USPS), and any other well-recognized company you may use.

When testing, make sure to test the logo position (top of page versus bottom, next to your order submit button, etc.).

http://www.i-cop.org/
http://www.honesteonline.com/
http://www.onlinebusinessbureau.com/
http://betterinternetbureau.com/
http://truste.com/
http://www.buysafe.com/
http://www.hackersafe.com/

Digital Product Security

Among Internet marketers, there's been an ongoing debate regarding digital product security.

There's no question that digital products are being copied and passed along to friends. What's even more troubling, though, is that some people will copy a product and put it on a file sharing site for anyone to download.

In fact, I recently had a client with a $2,000 digitally delivered product, and within days of his first sale, he found it on a file sharing site.

In another case, I discovered a site where the "members" decide what product they want, then they all chip in so *one* of them can purchase it. The purchasing member then duplicates the product and posts it online for the rest of the members to view.

You may find it interesting that this doesn't apply only to digital products—these people will take a paper-and-ink product, scan all of the pages, and post the digital copies online.

So, what's a merchant to do?

At one end of the spectrum, you have those who want to attach to every digital product the most onerous digital rights' management system they can find. Unfortunately, doing this will significantly increase your customer support requirements. I've never seen a digital antipiracy system that didn't cause some headaches for the end user.

At the other end of the spectrum are the people who don't do anything to stop the piracy, believing their time is better spent finding new marketing channels and creating new products. They consider digital piracy to be merely a cost of doing business.

My personal feelings are closer to this end of the spectrum. I think if someone is going to go searching for my product on the file sharing sites, they're probably not going to buy my product anyway. If they try to find my product on the file sharing sites and can't, they may buy my product, copy it, and return it—I'd rather they get it from the file sharing site and save us both the bother.

That being said, I do believe there's value in keeping the honest people honest, so some light-duty protection, such as a time-expiring download link, seems to make sense. Some of the following resources offer that kind of download mechanism, and some offer a bit more aggressive protection, but nothing too grievous to bear:

http://www.payloadz.com/
http://clicklocker.com/home.php

http://easyclickguard.com/
http://www.dlguard.com/dlginfo/index.php
http://www.locked-area.com/html/
http://www.softwaredefender.com/
http://www.cbprotect.com/
http://www.digdeliver.com

Direct Mail

I know what you're thinking—"Direct mail? Isn't this book supposed to be about *online* business?"

Believe it or not, direct mail is an integral component of many of the most successful online businesses.

In fact, "online business" can be somewhat of a misnomer. The Internet should be considered a *part* of your business, but you shouldn't limit yourself to using the Internet to the exclusion of all else. You should still talk to your prospects on the phone, and you should still use good old-fashioned postal mail.

In fact (and I know this suggestion will be quite shocking to some) you should even try to meet your clients face-to-face on occasion! I know it's a novel concept, but try it.

Now back to the subject at hand. Use direct mail to drive people to your site. As much as I love the ease of sending a message to 5,000 people at the click of a button, e-mail has its limitations.

It's getting blocked by the ISPs; it's getting blocked by the e-mail client spam filters; and it's getting lost in the crowd, becoming so much static in the lives of many of your prospects.

That's not to say it's dead, by any means . . . what I am saying is that limiting yourself to e-mail is limiting your profit potential in a big way.

What if you could send 5,000 real paper-and-ink *letters* with the click of a button? Do you think those 5,000 letters would have a little more impact sitting in your prospect's hand?

Is it possible that a simple piece of paper would have more impact than the subject line of your e-mail surrounded by a hundred other subject lines of other e-mails? (That's a rhetorical question.)

PRINT/MAIL POSTCARD SERVICES

Well, the great thing is that you *can* send 5,000 real paper-and-ink letters with the click of a button. It's not something you're going to do if you're strapped for cash, because you have to pay something for printing and mailing those letters— but not as much as you might think.

For instance, as of the writing of this book, I found one place that would print 5,000 postcards and mail them for $1,444 (including postage). The list rental would be another $500 or so. Just remember, it's not your marketing *cost* that matters—the return on investment is what you should be looking at.

Also remember, you don't have to start with 5,000 postcards. You could just send out 350 to your existing customers (who are likely going to be more responsive to your new offer in any case).

Here are some of the services that offer print/mail postcard services online:

http://amazingmail.com/
http://www.postcardpower.com/
http://www.sonicprint.com/
http://www.48hourprint.com/
http://www.fishdirectmail.com/ (USPS affiliate)
http://www.click2mail.com/ (USPS affiliate)
http://www.zairmail.com/

Another bonus: direct mail is very scalable, so once you have a proven winner, you can roll out in a big way (assuming you've chosen a big enough market).

AUTOMATED DIRECT MAIL FOLLOW-UP

Now this is so very cool from a marketing standpoint. Think of a marriage between an autoresponder service and direct mail. You can schedule any number of customer "touches" (communications) ahead of time, and they'll automatically go out without you giving it any more thought.

Once you get a customer, you would enter his or her information into the system. You'd already have a mailing profile that you'd attach this information to, and this would schedule:

A thank-you postcard three days later

A "here's a feature of your new widget you might enjoy" postcard four days after that

A birthday coupon five days before the customer's birthday

A Thanksgiving card

A monthly newsletter on a postcard, in addition to the preceding cards

. . . And more

With this company you can totally automate the nurturing of your customer relationships. It's like having a self-watering, self-weeding, self-fertilizing garden . . . check it out here:

http://www.sendOutCards.com/

While SendOutCards.com focuses on regularly sending out simple cards, these companies allow you to integrate several online and offline follow-up methods into a single follow-up campaign. These may include email, fax broadcasts, voice broadcasts, direct mail and more.

http://www.infusionsoft.com/
http://www.automatedmarketingsolutions.com/

DIRECT MAIL SERVICES

http://admsi.com/
http://www.zipmailusa.com/
http://www.gfxinc.com/
http://www.handymailing.com/

Also see the "Promotional Items and Incentives" for ideas about attention-grabbing items you can include in your direct mail campaigns.

MAIL LISTS AND LIST RESEARCH

http://www.srds.com/
http://www.oxbridge.com/
http://marketmodels.com/

ONLINE POSTAGE

http://www.netshipping.net

PHOTO STAMPS

These allow you to create your own postage stamp with any photo you choose, including your own:

http://www.zazzle.com/
http://www.stamps.com/
http://www.yourstamps.com/

Discussion Boards/Forums

Discussion boards have been around since before the Internet—you used to directly connect to a bulletin board system. Once connected, you could upload or download files and view/post messages to the other members.

The new term is *forum,* but the core concept is basically the same—a forum provides a place on your web site for people with similar interests to get together and exchange ideas and stories. New posts can be moderated and/or modified by the board administrator or assigned moderators.

Forums are one of the best ways to get free content from (and for) your web community. Once you have them set up and have a critical mass of active participants and posts, the forum becomes a self-sustaining search engine magnet. (I know that sounds like hype, but I'm not selling anything here!)

FORUM SOFTWARE

http://www.vbulletin.com/
http://www.wwwthreads.com/
http://awsd.com/scripts/webbbs/
http://www.simplemachines.org/

HOSTED FORUM SERVICES

http://www.ezforum.org/
http://www.network54.com/
http://www.proboards.com/
http://www.forumspring.com/
http://www.bravenet.com/

FORUM MONITORING

With these services, you can monitor the conversations taking place on forums:

http://www.boardtracker.com/
http://search.big-boards.com/
http://www.botsurfer.com/campbell/
http://www.forum-tracker.com/

FORUM SEARCH

You can search forums or browse forum categories on these two sites:

http://search.big-boards.com/
http://www.boardtracker.com/

DNS Services

A domain name server (DNS) is like an electronic web site address book. When you register a domain (e.g., "xyz.com"), you point it to a name server. You then tell the name server what IP address your web site will be using.

This is not as complicated as it sounds and is usually done for you by your hosting company if you're using a shared server, or from your web hosting manager if you're on a dedicated server.

Your name server then tells the rest of the known universe that it will be handling requests for your domain, and it also tells them what IP address has been assigned to that domain.

After that, when someone enters your web address in their browser location bar, here's what happens: The browser sends a query to your Internet service provider's name server asking, "Where can I find the xyz.com domain?" The name server replies with the IP address that your name server last broadcast.

Your browser then makes a connection to that IP address and requests the page the user has specified.

Your web server returns that page to your browser.

That's probably way more than you wanted to know about DNS (and that is a very simplified explanation), but

I've thrown it in here for those who may be curious about the technology involved.

Anyway, you can see that your name server is a critical component of the web infrastructure—if your name server goes down, nobody will know where to find your web site. So, if you want to make extra sure your web site is accessible, you can use multiple, geographically isolated name servers. Here are a couple of services that provide that functionality:

http://www.zoneedit.com/
http://www.easydns.com/

Domain Names

The domain name you select for your site can be as important as the title of a book or the name of a product—perhaps even more important when you take into account the search engines.

DOMAIN NAME SELECTION

Here are a few services that help you figure out a good domain name related to your site's target market or niche:

http://www.NameBoy.com/
http://www.makewords.com/
http://unique-names.com/word-mixer.php
http://domain-name-ideas.com/
http://ww.nametumbler.com/

DOMAIN REGISTRARS

http://www.000domains.com/
http://www.enom.com/
http://www.godaddy.com/

DELETED AND EXPIRED DOMAIN NAMES

Sometimes you can pick up a real gem of a domain name because someone bought it on speculation, couldn't get any money out of it, and allowed it to go back into the available domain name pool. The following services show you all of the recently expired or deleted domain names and allow you to claim them for yourself.

http://ww.bizmint.com/
http://www.snapcheck.com/
http://www.deleteddomains.com/
http://www.expireddomains.com/

If you're really lucky (or just patient), you can find an expired domain that still has some page rank in the search engines—bonus! Check out the services offered by these companies:

http://www.godaddy.com/
http://www.pool.com/
http://www.snapnames.com/

DOMAIN TOOLS

These allow you to find out information about existing domains (contact info, IP address, name servers, etc.):

http://www.domaintools.com/
http://www.dnsstuff.com/

Duplication

CD and DVD duplication is incredibly simple and inexpensive these days. Some of these offer fulfillment services as well. (See also "Fulfillment.")

http://kunaki.com/
http://www.starbyte.com/
http://www.discmakers.com/
http://www.blueridgedigital.com/
http://www.ioproducts.com/
http://www.arcal.com/
http://www.wts-tape.com/main.asp
http://www.cdduplicationcenter.com/pricing.html
http://www.disk.com/
http://www.proactionmedia.com/cd_duplication.htm
http://www.fulfillmentcentral.com/
http://profitspublishing.com/
http://www.goldenrom.com/
http://www.mcmannisduplication.com/

The Kunaki on-demand duplication and fulfillment service has become especially popular among Internet marketers, and a number of integration services are designed just for such marketers:

http://dvdautomator.com/
http://www.paypalkunaki.com/
http://kunakiautomator.com/
http://www.auctionacrobat.com/

eBay

When considering underutilized business tools, eBay must certainly rank near the top of the list. While most people still think of eBay as a place to sell your garage-sale leftovers, smart business owners are using eBay's huge traffic to their advantage.

One statistic I've heard bandied about recently is that people conduct more searches every day on eBay than they do on Google! I haven't been able to verify that particular claim, but from eBay's June 2008 stockholders' presentation, I do know it has 1 *billion* page views every day.

Additionally, eBay's "Marketplace Fast Facts" page states that it has 83.9 million *active* users.

What may be even more important is that the vast majority of eBay searches are done with the end goal of buying something! That makes this traffic significantly more valuable to the business owner than Google's.

Here, then, are some tools to help you make the most of eBay.

AUCTION AD SERVICE

http://www.aucads.com/

AUCTION CRM SYSTEM

http://www.auctioncontact.net/

eBAY AUCTION MANAGEMENT SOFTWARE

http://www.auctionsentry.com/

If you have digital products you want to sell on eBay, you will need to convert them to a tangible, deliverable format (e.g. burn it to a CD or DVD).

The "Auction Acrobat" software was designed specifically for eBay sellers who want to sell information products, and allows you to automate the digital-to-tangible conversion and delivery in conjunction with Kunaki.com

http://www.auctionacrobat.com/

ACCURATE PROFIT CALCULATOR

http://www.profitcalc.com/

SNIPING TOOL

This tool tracks the bids on an item of interest and enters your bid at the very end.

http://www.bidnapper.com

eBAY FINANCING

Did you know PayPal allows you to offer financing terms on certain purchases? This could help close some sales you would not otherwise get.

http://www.paypal.com/offercredit

AUCTION AUDIO

http://www.auctionaudio.net

LISTING SOFTWARE

Turbo Lister is eBay's free listing software program—it allows you to create and reuse various templates. It also allows you to schedule and automatically upload listings to eBay (this costs extra).

http://pages.ebay.com/turbo_lister/

WHOLESALE MERCHANDISE

"Buy low" is especially sound advice when looking for online auction merchandise. These companies allow you to purchase large quantities at low prices.

http://www.liquidation.com/
http://www.wholesalefinder.net

This is a bit of an arbitrage play—eBay owns half.com, where you can get name brand products at drastically reduced prices, so you can buy from half.com and sell on eBay!

http://www.half.com/

eBAY RESEARCH

This eBay research tool analyzes the last three months of data in any category you specify and then tells you all the important information, such as which products are selling, prices people are paying for those products, the best titles to use in your listings, and more. It's like having a crystal ball.

http://www.auctionresearchtool.com

eBAY PAGE STATS

This is a great tracking tool custom-designed for eBay. It will tell you how your visitors are finding your auction, what search terms they used to find it, how long they stayed, and more.

http://www.sellathon.com/

eBAY INTELLIGENCE

The old adage "Give them what they want" applies in eBay, too. This tool helps you select new items to sell by telling you what people are looking for.

http://www.auctionyen.com/

Keep in mind the auction format isn't the only way of selling on eBay. In fact, eBay's Fast Facts page showed that 42 percent of all sales were for fixed-price items ("Buy It Now").

The novelty of the auction model has worn off, and many people don't want to wait for an auction to end before they purchase the product. They just want to buy the dang thing and have it sent to them ASAP—this generation is *not* known for being patient.

eBAY CLASSIFIED ADS

For several eBay categories, you can even advertise with a fixed-price 30-day classified advertisement for just $9.95 (as of this writing).

As per traditional direct response, a business should not attempt to sell something directly from the classified ad. Instead, the advertisement is used to generate leads (offer a free report, a 10-point checklist, etc.), which you can then follow up and sell to later.

According to eBay (as of July 2008), the categories and subcategories for which classified advertisements can be placed are as follows:

Web Sites and Businesses for Sale
> Banner Ads, E-mail, Online * Radio, Television
> Text Links * Other Advertising Inventory * Home-based
> Businesses * Dating * Jewelry * Pet Supplies * Travel
> * Other * Entertainment * Hosting * Portals, Search *
> Other Internet Businesses * Manufacturing * Marketing
> * Patents, Trademarks * Retail, General Stores * Ser-
> vice Businesses * Vending, Coin-op * Wholesale Trade
> and Distribution * Other

Trade Show Booths
> Banner Systems, Signage * Pop-up and Booth Displays
> Tabletop and Portable Displays * Literature Stands and
> Racks * Trade Show Counters and Tables * Tradeshow

Booth Lighting * Travel and Carry Cases * Other Display Accessories * Other Trade Show Display

Prefabricated Buildings

Travel

Cruises * Lodging * Vacation Packages * Other Travel

Specialty Services

Everything Else

Advertising Opportunities * eBay User Tools * Funeral and Cemetery * Caskets * Cemetery Plots * Information Products * Memberships * Mystery Auctions * Impressions, Ad Space

E-Books

The term *e-book* can apply to just about any electronically distributed reading material that has been formatted as a book. The most popular and universally accessible e-book format is Adobe Acrobat's "Portable Document Format" (PDF), and there's an entire industry built around that particular format (see "PDF Resources" for more about it).

There are also a number of software packages that will take a collection of linked HTML pages and create an electronic book file in PC .exe format—these offer some nice presentation and security features, including the ability to lock the e-book to a particular computer and control user access to it (e.g., terminate access if a refund is requested).

The problem with these is their dependence on the Microsoft Windows operating system. Any potential customers who have a Mac or Linux system will be out of luck unless they have a Windows emulator program.

Still, some publishers are willing to make that sacrifice for the added features of the PC .exe format.

(Note: My earlier comments about digital security apply to e-books as well as other digital content.)

PC .exe E-BOOK-BUILDING TOOLS

If you want to create your own PC .exe e-book, here are a few tools to consider. Most of these require the e-book to be written in HTML (web pages) first, so please see "File Format Conversion" if you already have a book written in another format.

http://superwin.com/super.htm
http://www.ebookgenerator.com/
http://www.ebookpro.com/
http://www.ebookgold.com/
http://www.bersoft.com/hmhtml/
http://www.neosoftware.com/
http://www.x2net.com/webcompiler/
http://www.ebookedit.com/
http://www.bersoft.com/webpacker/

If you want to minimize your customer support requirements, I recommend you give strong consideration to distributing your e-books as PDF files—see "PDF Resources" for PDF-creation tools.

There are a number of services for creating e-book covers. You'll find these in "Graphics Design Services" and "E-book Cover Design Software" under "Graphics."

LISTING E-BOOKS IN AMAZON

Would you like to see your e-book listed at Amazon.com? Just send a blank e-mail to Amazon's autoresponder e-mail

address to get the ball rolling. Amazon will immediately reply
with instructions:

edoc-inquiry@amazon.com

E-BOOK DEVICES

In addition to e-books designed to be read on a personal
computer, there are now some hardware e-book platforms
such as the "Sony Reader" and the "Amazon Kindle."

http://ebookstore.sony.com/
http://kindle.amazon.com/

These hardware devices will hold from 80 to 200 books
in their proprietary format, and they also have the ability to
render PDF files on their displays (though not at the same
level of sharpness as you'll get on your computer). You can
purchase and download files wirelessly right from the readers
and store them on removable SD media cards.

E-Commerce Integrated Systems

These services typically combine most of the common functions in a tightly integrated system, including shopping carts, autoresponders, affiliate program functions, subscription systems, and digital product delivery systems.

These systems will give you the most bang for your buck—in some cases the flexibility isn't as great as with separate component systems, but there's less hassle involved.

http://www.infopia.com/
http://www.infusionsoft.com/
http://www.1shoppingcart.com/
http://www.memberspeed.com/
http://www.fantasos.com/
http://www.quickpaypro.com/
http://www.goldbar.net/
http://www.volusion.com/
http://www.synergyx.com/ (disclosure: I own this site)

Consider using a dedicated autoresponder–e-mail service when possible, even if your integrated system includes these functions.

The reason I say this is because, in my experience, the companies who focus on e-mail solutions have a better e-mail delivery rate.

E-Mail Marketing

The functionality offered by sequential autoresponder services and e-mail list management services are now overlapping to a point that they are indistinguishable. The services and software solutions listed here are advertised as e-mail list management, but many of them also have autoresponder capabilities.

Should you pay for a hosted service, or get your own software? Unfortunately, a growing number of legitimate subscribers are too lazy to click on the "unsubscribe" link in your e-mail, opting instead to hit the big red "Mark as spam" button.

With that in mind, I generally recommend using a hosted service, because these services maintain a relationship with the big ISPs (MSN, SBC-Yahoo!, AT&T, etc.) and can help you avoid being blacklisted due to the spurious spam allegations you *will* get from your users.

For the same reason, I recommend you use a confirmed opt-in model for acquiring your subscribers.

E-MAIL MARKETING HOSTED SERVICES

See also "Autoresponder Services/Software."

http://www.emaildirect.com/
http://www.instantservice.com
http://www.icontact.com
http://www.constantcontact.com/
http://www.ezinedirector.com/
http://www.ezinedesigner.com/
http://www.mailermailer.com/

If you're not going to use a hosted solution, there are a couple different options for managing an e-mail list yourself.

SERVER-BASED E-MAIL LIST SOFTWARE

If you want to send out e-mail from your own server, here are some software solutions you can choose from:

http://www.autoresponseplus.com/
http://www.phplist.com/
http://www.listmailpro.com/
http://www.greatcircle.com/majordomo/
http://www.infacta.com/
http://www.siteinteractive.com/subpro/

If you want to send it out from your own computer (not recommended for large lists), check out the solutions for PC-based e-mail that follow.

PC-BASED E-MAIL LIST SOFTWARE

http://www.postcast.com/
http://www.post-master.net/
http://www.extractorpro.com/
http://www.arialsoftware.com/emailmarketingdirector.htm
http://www.mailworkz.com/products.htm
http://www.gammadyne.com/mmail.htm
http://www.autoreplying.com/
http://www.mailloop.com/

HIGH-VOLUME E-MAIL MARKETING

If you're going to have very high e-mail volume (e.g., sending millions of e-mails), these are the solutions I'd recommend:

http://www.lsoft.com/
http://www.lyris.com
http://www.sparklist.com/

E-MAIL DELIVERY MONITORING

These services allow you to track the rate of "successful" delivery of your email to the large internet service providers.

http://www.e-filtrate.com/
http://www.deliverymonitor.com/

OTHER E-MAIL MARKETING RESOURCES

http://www.emailresults.com/directory_home.asp

E-Zines/ E-Letters

For all practical purposes, most electronic magazines (e-zines) are really just electronic newsletters . . . and they're usually as simple as a regularly scheduled broadcast from your e-mail list service.

However, if you give it the sexy moniker of *e-zine* instead of the drab label of *newsletter,* you get to promote it in the e-zine sites that follow. Score!

E-ZINE PROMOTION

http://www.ezine-queen.com/
http://www.ezineannouncer.com/

E-ZINE DIRECTORIES

http://www.ezine-dir.com/
http://www.ezinesearch.com/search-it/ezine/
http://new-list.com/
http://www.bestezines.com/
http://www.ezinehub.com/

File Format Conversion

Different applications on your computer require different file formats, and they don't always convert between the more common alternatives.

For converting between text, HTML, and PDF, check out these resources:

http://www.bcltechnologies.com/document/products/
    magellan/magellan.htm
http://doc2pdf.sourceforge.net/index.html
http://www.easysw.com/htmldoc/
http://www.pdfonline.com/
http://www.oakworth.demon.co.uk/gymnast.htm
http://www.fourthworld.com/products/webmerge/index
    .html
http://www.coolutils.com/Online-HTML-Converter.php
http://www.nativewinds.montana.com/software/tomahawk
    .html

For converting between different kinds of audio and video files, try these:

http://www.erightsoft.com/SUPER.html
http://www.coolutils.com/TotalMovieConverter/

For various other files (word processing documents, spreadsheet documents, image files, etc.), check out this nifty online power tool:

http://www.zamzar.com/

File Hosting

There may be times when you want to send a large file to someone, but it's too large to be sent via e-mail (I would generally discourage sending files larger than 5 megabytes via e-mail).

If you have your own web server, you can upload it and have the intended recipient download it from there. But if not, you can use one of these file hosting sites.

These are especially good if you want several people to download the files. Naturally you can password-protect the files so that the only people who can access them are those authorized by you.

These can also be used for quick-and-dirty off-site storage of your most important backup files.

http://www.sendmefile.com/howto.htm
http://www.box.net/
http://www.filesanywhere.com/
http://fileburst.com/
http://www.filesdirect.com/
http://yousendit.com/
http://www.dropload.com/
http://www.fileflow.com/
http://aws.amazon.com/ (click on "Simple Storage Service")

The last link in the preceding list is for Amazon's "Simple Storage Service" (S3), which *can* be used for simple file storage but is designed to do a lot more than that. S3 allows you to off-load bandwidth-intensive content from your server to Amazon's servers. This helps you reduce the load on your own server while at the same time helping you avoid bandwidth overage charges.

Because you're using Amazon's servers, your bandwidth scaling is virtually unlimited—so if you're expecting a great deal of traffic for a particular promotion, this can save you from the embarrassment of a server crash.

S3 is typically used to host and serve video components, but you can use it to store and deliver any kind of file.

In fact, for one client who was expecting extremely heavy traffic to a time-sensitive promotion, I loaded his sales page and all of its associated images and video files to S3. I then set up the page on his web server to merely frame that page. Doing it this way, each request required his server to deliver only a tiny 401-byte frame page, while Amazon's servers were delivering 122,000 bytes *plus* several megabytes for each video that was activated.

Amazon's storage and bandwidth fees are very reasonable— to store files totaling 1 gigabyte costs only 15 cents per month, and delivering 100 gigabytes of bandwidth (enough for 1 million page views of a 100,000-byte file) would cost just $17.00—and you pay for only what you use; there are no monthly minimum fees.

Keep in mind that it's not a good strategy from a search engine standpoint to have your home page hosted at

Amazon, but you can certainly have any embedded videos hosted there.

After you get an Amazon Web Services account and sign up for S3, you will need software to move files between your computer and Amazon's. You can use the free S3Fox Firefox extension (see the next section, "Firefox Extensions"), or you can use commercial software. One such application is here:

http://www.otakusoftware.com/upright/

Firefox Extensions

The Firefox browser has a robust extension system whereby anyone can create a small program that runs in the browser. There are thousands of add-ons of every conceivable kind (almost 8,000 as of this writing).

Here are some examples of what's available:

Grab Them All
> https://addons.mozilla.org/en-US/firefox/addon/7800
>
> Captures web sites as a screen capture—batch processing allows you to capture all the sites listed in a simple text file and store the images to a specified folder on your computer.

S3Fox
> https://addons.mozilla.org/en-US/firefox/addon/3247
>
> Interfaces with the Amazon S3 file storage service, allowing you to upload and download files there.

Gspace
> https://addons.mozilla.org/en-US/firefox/addon/1593
>
> This extension allows you to use your Gmail Space (4.1 gigabytes and growing) for file storage.

It acts as an online drive, so you can upload files from your hard drive and access them from every Internet-capable system.

ReminderFox (reminder utility)

https://addons.mozilla.org/en-US/firefox/addon/1191

PDF Download

https://addons.mozilla.org/en-US/firefox/addon/636

Alerts you when you click a PDF link and gives you the option of viewing it in the browser or saving it to your hard drive.

GA? ("Google Analytics?")

https://addons.mozilla.org/en-US/firefox/addon/5631

Checks to see whether Google Analytics is installed on current web page.

BlogRovr

https://addons.mozilla.org/en-US/firefox/addon/4689

RovR fetches posts from your favorite blogs about anything you're browsing and shows you summaries; you can open and read posts without leaving the web page you're on.

Extended Status (page load status bar)

https://addons.mozilla.org/en-US/firefox/addon/1433

CraigZilla

https://addons.mozilla.org/en-US/firefox/addon/6288

Integrates CraigsList into Firefox.

AlexaSparky (Get Alexa data on your status bar.)

https://addons.mozilla.org/en-US/firefox/addon/5362

Google Preview

https://addons.mozilla.org/en-US/firefox/addon/189

Inserts screenshot images in your Google and Yahoo! search results

Window Resizer

https://addons.mozilla.org/en-US/firefox/addon/1985

Lets you see how your web site looks to people with different screen sizes.

SEOQuake

https://addons.mozilla.org/en-US/firefox/addon/3036

Gives you search engine–related data for the current web site.

CoolIris Previews

https://addons.mozilla.org/en-US/firefox/addon/2207

When you mouse over a link, a preview (screenshot) of that page is shown.

Download Them All

https://addons.mozilla.org/en-US/firefox/addon/201

This is a download manager, allowing you to accelerate, pause and resume downloads.

Flash Tools

Adobe's Flash technology is used for adding animation, video feeds, text effects, and even small web applications.

Fortunately for most of us, you don't need to be a bona fide Flash MX programmer to accomplish some impressive things—there's an ever-growing market of third-party tools that do most of the work for you.

Now, you aren't going to have the same level of control and functionality as the geek squad has with their Flash tools, but I think you'll be surprised with what you can do, and how quickly.

http://flashpublishers.com/
http://www.flashguru.co.uk/
http://www.flashkit.com/
http://www.flashpublishers.com/
http://www.swishzone.com/

Fulfillment

So you have a web site selling physical, shippable products. If you don't have your own shipping department (and don't want one), you can use these companies to take care of both inbound and outbound fulfillment.

You simply send the order details and they will pack and ship your product to the customer. If you are selling information products, some of these companies may also offer print-on-demand services.

http://bvivid.com/index.html
http://www.disk.com/
http://www.speakerfulfillmentservices.com/
http://directtomarketsolutions.com/
http://www.deliveryourbooks.com/
http://www.webgistix.com/
http://www.wefulfillit.com/
http://www.expressfulfillment.com/Fulfillment.htm
http://www.FillOrders.com/
http://www.vervante.com/

See also "Print on Demand" under "Printing."

Google

Everyone knows about Google's search functions, but the company has a number of lesser-known yet extremely useful tools known as "Google Services."

Google Base allows you to submit any kind of data for inclusion in Google's search results. This can include items for sale, recipes, job descriptions, personal ads—literally anything.

You can include attributes to help people find your listings when they do relevant searches:

http://base.google.com/

If you have a lot of items to list for sale, you can use this software to create a "bulk upload" file in conformance with Google Base's API:

http://www.siteall.com/

Google Product Search is a product search engine—items that you submit via Google Base may appear in Google Product Search if they are relevant to the user's search:

http://www.google.com/products/

Google Webmaster Tools is a collection of tools designed to help you with several aspects of your web site, including:

Google Sitemaps for informing Google of content you want indexed

Google Analytics to analyze your site traffic and effectiveness

Google Optimizer for testing various elements of your web site (multivariate testing)

And more . . .

All of these tools are free, and some of these tools are comparable to commercial software costing thousands of dollars:

http://www.google.com/webmasters/

In addition to the Google Sitemap generation tool provided by Google, here are three software tools for creating Google sitemaps:

http://www.sitemapdoc.com/
http://www.sourceforge.net/projects/goog-sitemapgen
http://gsitecrawler.com/

Every webmaster should become familiar with Google's own published guidelines, recommendations, and how-to instructions—these are organized in a simple-to-follow "Frequently Asked Questions" format.

https://www.google.com/support/webmasters/?hl=en

Google Catalogs (see scanned images of various mail-order
   catalogs):
      http://catlogs.google.com/

To see additional tools and follow the newest develop-
ments, check out Google Labs.

   http://labs.google.com/

Also check out Google's "options" page to see several of
the other services it offers:

   http://www.google.com/intl/en/options/

For Google AdWords, see "Pay-per-Click (PPC) Search
Engines." For Google search engine optimization, see
"Search Engine Optimization."

Graphics

While the words on your site sell, the graphics play an important supporting role. Unless you are a graphics designer yourself, you have two choices: (1) License existing graphics, or (2) have graphics designed exclusively for your use.

GRAPHICS CREATION AND EDITING SOFTWARE

For graphics design and editing, the market leader has long been Adobe Photoshop. Paint Shop Pro is also popular, as is Xara Xtreme.

http://www.adobe.com/products/photoshop/
http://www.corel.com/PaintShopPro/
http://xara.com/us/

Besides these commercial applications, there are a number of good free solutions:

http://www.irfanview.com/
http://www.gimp.org/windows/
http://www.freeserifsoftware.com/software/PhotoPlus/
http://www.freeserifsoftware.com/software/DrawPlus/

GRAPHICS TUTORIALS

For those who want to do it themselves and need a little instruction, there are some online tutorials to help:

http://www.good-tutorials.com/
http://graphicreporter.com/
http://www.designtutorials.info/

CARTOON LICENSING

To license cartoons for your site or printed publication, check out these sites:

http://www.kingfeatures.com/reprint/index.htm
http://www.cartoonbank.com/pro_index.asp
http://www.glasbergen.com/
http://www.Toon-a-Day.com/
http://www.cartoonlink.com/

PHOTOGRAPH LICENSING

You can also license photographs from several stock photography companies. Licensing for commercial use can cost as little as $1.00 for a low-resolution photo—or can even be had for free in some cases (with some restrictions).

http://www.photodisc.com/
http://www.shutterstock.com/
http://www.istockphoto.com/
http://www.fotosearch.com/

http://www.comstock.com/
http://www.photos.com/
http://www.hemera.com/
http://www.sxc.hu/ (free)
http://www.freefoto.com/

GRAPHICS DESIGN SERVICES

Most of these are billed as "e-book cover" designers, but I know at least some of them will do other graphics work for your web site as well.

http://killercovers.com/
http://absolutecovers.com/
http://privatelabelsales.com/custom_designs.htm
http://www.hidefcovers.com/
http://www.ecoverfx.com/
http://www.ebookgraphics.com/
http://www.gotlogos.com/
http://bannersmall.com/
http://www.romegraphics.com/

E-BOOK COVER DESIGN SOFTWARE

If you want to create your own e-book covers, you can get software to do most of the heavy lifting:

http://www.coverfactory.com/
http://www.ecovertools.com/
http://www.webgraphicscreator.com/
http://www.cover-action-pro.com

BOOK COVER DESIGN

If you have a real paper-and-ink book, this service does great book cover design (check out its ISBN and bar code service, too):

http://aardvarkglobalpublishing.com/cover_design.php

3D RENDERING AND ANIMATION SOFTWARE

If you want to go to the next level of visual impact on your site, check out what's possible with 3D rendering and animation software. The advanced simulation capabilities available on your computer today are amazing—especially when you consider the low cost of entry.

In fact, the Vue software at e-onsoftware.com was used for scenes in *Pirates of the Caribbean II* and *The Spiderwick Chronicles*. Simply incredible stuff. The learning curve will be steep, though, so unless you're into this kind of thing, plan on outsourcing the work.

http://my.smithmicro.com/win/poser/index.html
http://www.daz3d.com/
http://www.pandromeda.com/products/
http://www.maxon.net/pages/products/products_e.html
http://www.e-onsoftware.com/products/
http://freeserifsoftware.com/software/3dPlus/default.asp

For royalty-free video content, see "Video."

Help Desk Software

If you're going to have any significant sales volume, you can plan on having an equally significant volume of customer support requests. And unless you have full-time support staff manning the phones, you need to provide other ways for people to contact you online.

There was a time when a "support" e-mail (e.g., support@example.com) that would be directed to your support staff was sufficient and even preferred—but not anymore.

The problem now is that e-mail is just too unreliable to be used for something as important as customer support—too great a chance that you'll not receive customers' help requests or that they won't receive your reply.

I now recommend the use of help desk "ticket system" software. Personally, I'd rather just send an e-mail and be done with it. But I have resigned myself to the reality that my help request is more likely to be seen and responded to if I'm submitting it through help desk software.

http://www.omnihelpdesk.com/index.html
http://www.osticket.com/

http://www.perldesk.com/
http://www.readydesk.com/
http://www.bestpractical.com/rt/
http://www.deskpro.com/
http://www.cerberusweb.com/
http://www.kayako.com/

JavaScript

JavaScript is the scripting language that controls most of today's popular web browsers. It can be used in a number of ways, including:

Validating online form data prior to submitting it your server

Setting and reading browser cookies

Sending your browser to a different page

Opening new browser windows

Text and image effects

Loading new content without changing the page

Displaying syndicated content from other sites

Online calculators (financial, calorie counters, etc.)

Calendar functions

HTML editors

Much more!

If you browse these JavaScript repositories, you will find scores of interesting functions that you can quickly add to your own web pages—many are free but require you to preserve copyright or other attributing language.

http://www.hotscripts.com/
http://www.dynamicdrive.com/
http://javascript.internet.com/

Keywords

When I talk about keywords here, I'm talking about the words and phrases you focus on when promoting your site, as well as the words and phrases people use when searching for (and finding) your site. These two sets of keywords aren't always the same!

For search engine optimization, you want to make sure your site comes up on one of the first search engine pages (number one if possible, naturally) when users search for keywords most relevant to your site's theme.

For pay-per-click search engine advertising, you will want to generate a list of all the relevant keywords and keyword phrases. Some of these will be profitable and some won't, but you won't know which are which until you start advertising with them. As you determine the unprofitable keywords, you can remove them from your account and raise your bid prices for the profitable ones. See "Pay-Per-Click (PPC) Search Engines" for more information about this.

Keyword selection should also be an integral part of any of your "article marketing" efforts.

These tools help you select keywords to bid on, generate keyword lists, and analyze your site's keyword performance (and that of other sites as well).

https://adwords.google.com/select/KeywordToolExternal
http://www.goodkeywords.com/
http://www.keyworddensity.com/
http://www.digitalpoint.com/tools/suggestion/
http://www.keyword-toolkit.com/
http://www.wordtracker.com/
http://freekeywords.wordtracker.com/ (free version)
http://www.boxersoftware.com/thepermutator.htm
http://www.KeywordWorkshop.com/
http://www.keywordcountry.com/
http://www.keywordselite.com/
http://www.keyworddomination.com/
http://www.keywordmax.com/
http://www.topkeywordlists.com/rss/news.xml
http://www.keywordelite.com/
http://freekeywords.wordtracker.com/

Leads

Once you have proven the profitability of your sales process, you can consider purchasing leads on a large scale.

These companies provide leads for outbound phone and direct mail sales. Leads can be selected based on your required demographics.

http://www.goleads.com/
http://www.infousa.com/
http://www.experianb2b.com/landp/index.html
http://www.venteinc.com/
http://www.smartclicks.com/about.html
http://salesgenie.com/
http://www.sponsera.com/
http://responsiveleads.com/
http://www.goleadsbusiness.com/
http://www.Lookupusa.com/
http://directleads.com

Legal

No legal advice here—I'm not an attorney! But definitely check out these resources for Web-related legal issues.

Copyright monitoring
  http://www.copyscape.com/
Copyright service
  http://www.clickandcopyright.com/
Trademarks
  http://www.nameprotect.com/index.html
Copyright attorneys
  http://www.hynak.com/
Web site legal disclaimers
  http://www.internet-law-compliance.com/
  http://websitelegalforms.com/
Fighting digital piracy:
  http://cybercrimeinvestigator.com/

Note: The only way to really be safe is to have your attorney (preferably one familiar with Internet-related law) review any legal documents before you put them on your site or send them out.

The one attorney I've worked with and can recommend is Bob Silber:

http://www.internetmarketinglawproducts.com/

Link Directories/ Portals

If you have a bunch of resource links you want to organize in a directory on your web site (similar to the Yahoo! directory), these software packages will do it for you.

http://www.in-portal.net/in-link/
http://gonafish.com/linkscaffepro.php
http://www.phpwebscripts.com/linkupgold/
http://www.dynaportal.com/

Also consider the CMS applications listed under "Content Management"—this kind of thing should be a piece of cake for those systems.

Marketing Forums and Newsletters

I believe effective marketing will have a greater impact on your business success than anything else. These forums are great for bouncing ideas off of other business owners and finding out what's working for them.

http://www.marketingbestpractices.com/forum/
http://www.ducttapemarketing.com/forum/
http://www.ablakeforum.com/
http://www.sowpub.com/
http://www.warriorforum.com/
http://www.clickbanksuccessforum.com/forum/

The newsletters will greatly expand your knowledge and will give you new ideas to try out in your own business.

http://www.undergroundsecretsociety.com/
http://www.marketingletter.com/
http://www.marketingexperiments.com/

http://marketingbestpractices.com/newsletter.htm
http://www.talkbiznews.com/
http://www.kingofcopy.com/ssnl/
http://www.imnewswatch.com/

I especially recommend Dan Kennedy's "No B.S. Marketing Letter":

http://nobsfreegift.com/offer/

Media Hosting

If your web site includes audio or video presentations, you may want to host the audio and video elsewhere for better performance.

One option is Amazon's S3 service (discussed earlier), but there are several other services that specialize in delivering a high volume of high-bandwidth content, and these may provide better performance to your site visitors. (Though I've never had a problem myself just using Amazon S3, I haven't done any extremely high volume.)

http://www.techsmith.com/screencast.asp/
http://www.streamingmediahosting.com/
http://video.google.com/
http://www.zippyvideos.com/
http://www.vitalstream.com/hosting/index.html
http://www.hipcast.com/
http://youtube.com/
http://www.trafficgeyser.com/
http://streamhoster.com/
http://www.veoh.com/

http://www.viddler.com/
http://www.instantvideomachine.com/
http://www.dropshots.com/
http://www.photobucket.com/
http://tinypic.com/

Membership Site Software

Membership programs are great for maintaining a steady flow of recurring revenue, and the number of available membership management systems increases every day.

http://www.amember.com/
http://memberstar.com/
http://www.membershipclientpro.com/
http://www.membergate.com/ (Windows + ColdFusion)
http://www.siteinteractive.com/acctman/
http://www.passwordrobot.com/
http://www.interlogy.com/
http://www.easymemberpro.com/
http://www.instantmember.com/

See also "E-commerce Integrated Systems," as some of those services also provide membership features.

Some of the CMS systems under "Content Management" probably have plug-ins available to enable this same kind of functionality.

Merchant Accounts

In order to process credit card payments, you need a credit card merchant account. Setting up one of these used to be an expensive and difficult endeavor, but now it's much easier.

Once you have an account, you need to follow all the rules, because if you're ever put on the "terminated merchants" list, you'll have almost no chance of getting another one. In fact, it's a good idea to have multiple merchant accounts and multiple payment gateway accounts so that if you have problems with one, you can quickly switch your web site to the other.

These companies can get you set up with a merchant account and a payment gateway quickly and with a minimum of hassle. I have used MerchantExpress myself and have had clients use this company with good success as well.

http://www.merchantexpress.com/
http://www.charge.com/
http://www.ipowerpay.com/

SIDE NOTE

Just for clarification—a payment gateway is separate from your merchant account.

The gateway sits between your web site and your merchant account—when a payment request comes in through your e-commerce software, the payment gateway gets the approval from the credit card network and tells your system to proceed with the order processing.

At the end of each day, it settles the transactions with the network, and the funds are deposited a few days later in the bank account tied to your merchant account.

Currently, iPowerPay is developing a reputation as the merchant account provider of choice for people who will be having high-volume (six-plus figures) spikes in a short period of time.

Some of my clients have had their credit card volume running at a few thousand dollars a month and then suddenly shoot up to $2.5 million in a single day. (I wish I could say it was because of something I did, but alas, that's not the case!)

These kinds of things make most merchant account providers very nervous—they're afraid you'll empty your bank account and skip town, leaving them to pay thousands of dollars in refunds from defrauded consumers.

Unfortunately for the legitimate marketer, all too often the merchant account provider will have a knee-jerk reaction, shutting down the merchant account and holding the funds for a few months.

If you're going to have those kinds of spikes, be sure you talk to your merchant account provider first. Let your provider know it's coming and exactly what you're going to be selling, your promotion plan, and so on. Your provider just wants to be sure there's not some kind of scam going on.

And it wouldn't hurt to get a backup account from iPowerPay, just to be safe.

Mind Mapping Software

Mind mapping is a centuries-old technique frequently used to organize information for brainstorming, visualization, classification, and problem solving.

Basically, you take a central idea and arrange related words or pictures around it, linking them together as they relate to each other. These applications remove the mechanical inefficiencies of the past and allow you to focus your energy on the organization.

http://www.mindjet.com/us/
http://sourceforge.net/projects/freemind/
http://freemind.sourceforge.net/
http://www.gemx.com/doorganizer.php
http://www.imindmap.com/

Miscellaneous Resources

Some of the most useful tools in this book are in this section—
they just don't fall nicely into the other categories, so I've put
them into this catchall.

AD SERVER

http://www.adjuggler.com/
http://www.spinbox.com/
http://www.openx.org/

AD SERVING SERVICE

http://www.adbutler.com/
http://www.adspeed.com/
http://www.discountclick.com/adserving.asp

AMAZON LISTING: GET YOUR PRODUCTS LISTED ON AMAZON

http://advantage.amazon.com/gp/vendor/public/join-
advantage-books

APPOINTMENT SCHEDULING

http://www.flashappointments.com/
http://www.web-appointments.com/

BLACKLIST CHECKER

http://rbls.org/

See whether your web site is on an email blacklist.

BOOKMARK MANAGER

http://www.kaylon.com/power.html

I use this one and highly recommend it!

http://www.surfulater.com/

This is actually a lot more than a bookmark manager—
it allows you to save text and images from web pages in a
hierarchical structure of "articles." You can then do text
searches across all articles. Excellent for saving pages relevant
to your online research.

BUSINESS CHARTS SOFTWARE

http://smartdraw.com/

COMPUTERS, SOFTWARE AND ELECTRONICS

http://www.dell.com/
http://www.tigerdirect.com/

http://www.newegg.com/
http://www.ecost.com/

Be sure to check out the bargain countdowns at ecost.com!

CONTEST/DRAWING SOFTWARE

http://www.prizedrawgenerator.com/

DATABASES (HOSTED)

http://www.quickbase.com/
http://www.myowndb.com/
http://www.weboffice.com/
http://www.caspio.com/

FREEFORM DATABASE SOFTWARE (PC)

http://www.askSam.com/
http://www.wjjsoft.com/

DATABASE TO HTML

http://fourthworld.com/products/webmerge/index.html

DATA RECOVERY SOFTWARE

Even if you back up religiously, you may still need to recover corrupted data files written since the last backup . . . that's what these tools are for.

http://www.r-tt.com/
http://www.grc.com/sr/spinrite.htm

DIRECT MARKETING NEWS

http://www.napco.com/
http://www.dmnews.com/
http://www.the-dma.org/
http://www.directmag.com/

DOCUMENT CONVERSION

http://www.bookscanning.com/
http://www.discountdocumentscanning.com/

DOWNLOAD SITES

Just about any kind of software can be downloaded on a trial basis (e.g., shareware)—if you like it, you can pay to continue using it, and if you don't like the software, it hasn't cost you anything.

http://downloads.zdnet.com/
http://www.download.com/
http://www.tucows.com/

E-LEARNING SOFTWARE

http://www.eclass.net/
http://www.articulate.com/
http://www.joomlalms.com/
http://www.adobe.com/resources/elearning/

E-MAIL TO FAX

http://www.faxitnice.com/
http://www.faxaway.com/rates.shtml

EXCEL TEMPLATES AND FORMULAS

http://www.ozgrid.com/

HTML ENCRYPTION

http://www.iwebtool.com/html_encrypter
http://www.aw-soft.com/htmlguard.html

HTTP SNIFFER SERVICE

http://web-sniffer.net/

HTTP SNIFFER SOFTWARE

http://www.httpsniffer.com/

INTERNET MARKETING SEMINAR

http://www.UndergroundOnlineSeminar.com/

There are many, but in my opinion this is the best.

ISBN NUMBERS

http://www.isbn.org/
http://aardvarkglobalpublishing.com/isbn_numbers.php

LOCAL BUSINESS LISTINGS

http://yellowpages.com/

MARKETING EDUCATION (FREE)

http://www.hardtofindseminars.com/
http://www.internetmarketingcourse.com/

MEDIA LABELS

http://www.onlinelabels.com/labeltypecdrom.htm

MLM SOFTWARE

http://www.dhsoftwares.com/products/index.php
http://www.envex.com/

NEWS AGGREGATOR

http://www.moreover.com/

ORGANIZER

http://www.treepad.com/

PASSWORD VAULT

http://keepass.info/

PAYPAL IPN ASSISTANT

http://worldwidecreations.com/paypal_assistant.htm

PAYROLL SERVICE

If you're still doing your own payroll accounting, you'll be surprised at the low cost to liberate yourself. Check out these payroll services, and quit sweating those quarterly tax forms!

http://www.surepayroll.com/
http://adp.com/
http://www.paychex.com/
http://payroll.intuit.com/
http://www.cspayroll.com/
http://www.paycycle.com/
http://www.paychex.com/

PHONE RECORDER

http://www.usbrecorder.com/

PORTABLE WORD PROCESSOR

http://www.alphasmart.com/Retail/

PRODUCT SOURCES

http://worldwidebrands.com/

REMOTE PC ACCESS

http://www.gotomypc.com/
http://www.logmein.com/ (free option!)

ROBOTS.TXT CHECKER

http://tool.motoricerca.info/robots-checker.phtml

SHAREWARE PROMOTION

http://www.aidsoft.com/

SIGNATURE VALIDATION

http://signaturelink.com/

START YOUR OWN SOCIAL NETWORK

http://www.dzoic.com/
http://www.ning.com/

SPEED-READING IN 16 MINUTES

http://www.xonemarketing.com/SpeedReading/

SECURE SSL CERTIFICATES

http://www.geotrust.com/
http://www.thawte.com/
http://www.verisign.com/
http://www.godaddyssl.com/

SHORT LINK SERVICES

http://www.tinyurl.com/
http://www.snipurl.com/
http://www.shorterlink.com/
http://www.metamark.net/

SURGE SUPPRESSORS

http://www.brickwall.com/ (the only ones I trust)

TASK MANAGEMENT SOFTWARE

http://www.gemx.com/doorganizer.php

TELEPHONE ANSWERING/ ORDER-TAKING SERVICES

http://www.ntas.com/
http://www.liveops.com/
http://www.answerquick.com

TEXT EDITORS

http://www.boxersoftware.com/
http://www.notetab.com/
http://www.ultraedit.com/
http://www.notepad-plus.sourceforge.net/uk/site.htm
http://www.editplus.com/

http://www.textpad.com/index.html
http://www.pspad.com/
http://www.liquidninja.com/metapad/

TIME BILLING

http://www.ether.com/

TRANSCRIPTION SERVICES

http://www.escriptionist.com/
http://www.hiredhand.com/
http://www.GetItTranscribed.com/
http://www.successtranscripts.com/
http://www.idictate.com/
http://www.enablr.com/
http://www.andersontranscriptionservices.com/

E-MAIL-TO-PRINTED-LETTER SERVICE

http://enablr.com/stenographr.php

BROWSER TOOLBAR BUILDERS

http://www.freecustomtoolbar.com/
http://createtoolbar.com/

TRANSLATION

http://www.vonkempelen.com/

VIRTUAL OFFICE

http://www.afteroffice.com/
http://www.groove.net/

VOICE BROADCASTING

http://www.AutomaticResponse.com/
http://www.easyivr.com/

VOICE OVER IP

These are computer phone services and related software.

http://www.skype.com/
http://www.extras.skype.com/
http://www.gizmoproject.com/
http://www.pamela-systems.com/
http://www.hotrecorder.com/
http://www.solicall.com/
http://www.skylook.biz/

WEB MAIL

http://www.gmail.com/
http://www.mail.yahoo.com/
http://www.hotmail.com/

WINDOWS CLIPBOARD EXTENDER

http://www.smartcode.com/software.htm

WRITING SOFTWARE

http://www.smartauthor.com/

WEB SITE INTERACTION TOOLS

http://www.bravenet.com/
http://www.onyoursite.com/
http://www.SiteGadgets.com/

Newsletter Services

A monthly printed newsletter is one of the best ways you can keep "touching" your customers.

The idea is to keep your company in their minds—that way, when they're ready to get whatever it is you sell, you will be the only company they think of.

The following sources will create a monthly printed newsletter for you with a number of articles and tips.

You can customize the newsletter to include your own monthly coupon or promotional offer before you send it out to your customers.

http://www.internetviz.com/services.htm
http://www.garponline.com/
http://www.petetheprinter.com/done4you.pdf

Outsourcing

One of the keys to being a successful business owner is to focus your time on the things only you can do.

Say you're drawing a salary of $100,000 per year from your business. For a 52-week year, working 40 hours a week, that means your time is worth $48 an hour.

I know what you're thinking—for business owners, a 40-hour week is about as real as mermaids and unicorns, right? But use the resources in this section and you may actually have a shot at making it real.

Now, think about the things you do in a typical day. Are you spending time futzing around with your web site, getting things "just right"? How much time do you spend cleaning the junk out of your e-mail in-box? Are you personally answering customer support questions about billing and fulfillment?

You know where this is leading: How much of your $48 hourly time do you spend doing jobs worth $10 per hour?

The efficiencies of the Internet have given rise to a myriad of companies that will do those $10 an hour jobs for you—and because of the money value in different economies, the same kind of work can often be had for much less than $10 an hour.

For instance, I just did a quick check and found one off-shore company offering various services for under $5 per hour.

A word of caution here: The quality of work, speed of completion, and communications ability of the people employed by these companies will vary. So it's a good idea to hire two or three people at first and give them small and simple tasks to start out.

As providers complete projects to your satisfaction, you can give them more complex assignments.

http://www.elance.com/
http://www.guru.com/
http://www.rentacoder.com/
http://www.odesk.com/
http://www.scriptlance.com/
http://www.ossweb.com/ (proofing)
http://www.agentsofvalue.com/ (full-time staff)
http://www.FreelancersDirect.com/
http://www.vonkempelen.com/
http://www.trafficassistants.com/
http://www.allfreelancework.com/
http://www.freelanceworkexchange.com/
http://www.mturk.com/mturk/welcome/
http://www.editingandwritingservices.com/

CUSTOMER SUPPORT

If you're looking specifically to outsource your customer support, these companies specialize in that kind of service:

http://customerdirect.com/
http://peoplesupport.com/

http://egain.com/
http://www.livesalesman.com/
http://www.brigade.com/
http://www.shieffservices.com/index.html

VIRTUAL ASSISTANTS

http://www.SignatureWorx.com/
http://execadminsolutions.com/
http://keysupportservices.com/
http://www.suburbanofficeservices.com/
http://www.workaholics4hire.com/

P3P Policies

This is quite decidedly a step across the geek line, but important enough that I'm including it here. First, you need some background information on browser cookies.

A *cookie* is a small file written to your hard drive. It allows a web site to store information about you or your browsing session on that site. Generally, this is used to personalize the web site with your preferences.

For instance, on your first visit to a weather site, you might be asked to enter your zip code to check the weather. The next time you come to the same site, it will read your zip from the cookie it had previously sent—thus it can take you directly to the current weather outlook for your area.

Any time you return to a site that already knows your name, zip code, or some similar information, it's because your browser previously accepted a cookie from that site.

If you disable cookies in your web browser, many of your most popular sites will probably stop working in the same manner as they had before—this is because, without cookies, they can only assume you're a first-time visitor and can show you only the default information (with nothing customized to your previously set preferences).

Virtually all retail sites also use cookies to keep track of the items you've added to your shopping cart—many simply won't work without cookies being enabled.

Now, with that background, let's get back to P3P.

The Platform for Privacy Preferences Project (P3P) defines a "compact privacy policy," which is a type of shorthand privacy policy your web server can be configured to send with every response (e.g., for every requested web page or image).

Some of today's web browsers (including Internet Explorer) evaluate a site's compact privacy policy—coupled with the user-specified security level—to determine whether or not to accept a cookie from that site.

Thus, if your site isn't sending a P3P compact privacy policy, some visitors may have problems with your shopping cart system, membership or community area, or other interactive areas of your site.

Here are some tools for creating the required P3P policy files, as well as some validation and analysis tools.

P3P POLICY GENERATORS

http://www.p3pwiz.com/
http://www.p3pprivacy.com/
http://p3pedit.com/

P3P VALIDATOR

http://www.w3.org/P3P/validator.html

P3P DOCUMENTATION

http://www.w3.org/P3P/

To see other sites' machine-readable P3P compact policies and what they mean, use this tool.

P3P COMPACT POLICY ANALYZER

http://www.paulgalloway.com/utilities/p3p-analyze.cgi

Pay-Per-Click (PPC) Search Engines

I remember back in 1999, one of my clients told me about this outrageous idea some no-name search engine had. They were going to actually charge people money to be listed in their search engine! I mean, who would pay to be in a search engine when all the other search engines would list you for free? Crazy right?

(Sigh . . .)

That company was Goto.com, later to become Overture. com, and now Yahoo! Sponsored Search—and its "crazy" idea changed the face of Internet marketing.

For the uninitiated, pay-per-click ads are those little ads you see on the right side of your browser whenever you do a search at Google, Yahoo!, or any of other site with search functions powered by one of the PPC search engines. PPC ads were originally limited to text, but now just about every kind of ad format is supported, including audio and video ads.

If you click on the link for one of those ads, the advertiser is charged a fee for that click. The amount they pay is determined by a complex algorithm that takes into account the maximum bid set by the advertiser and the performance of the advertisement.

The most popular PPC search engine by far is Google AdWords—though it started out behind Goto.com by more than a year, AdWords was a much more efficient system for the advertiser. This, coupled with the popularity Google already enjoyed as a search engine, helped it quickly become the dominant player in the marketplace, and it continues to hold that position.

The foremost reason PPC advertising is such a powerful tool for marketing is speed of execution.

Setting up an advertising campaign can be done in just a few minutes, and once that campaign is activated, you can start receiving traffic almost instantaneously. You can also set up multiple advertisements for the same keywords and split-test them. This allows you to quickly find the highest-converting combination of keywords, title copy, and body copy.

The PPC search engines also provide you with the tracking tools necessary to determine the ROI of your advertising. You may find that one advertisement gives you a better click conversion, but another with a lower click conversion actually results in more revenue per dollar spent.

MOST POPULAR PPC SEARCH ENGINES

http://adwords.google.com/
http://sem.smallbusiness.yahoo.com/searchenginemarketing/
http://advertising.msn.com/microsoft-adcenter

http://www.kanoodle.com/
http://www.7search.com/
http://www.searchfeed.com/

PPC SEARCH ENGINES REVIEWED

http://www.payperclicksearchengines.com/
http://www.payperclickanalyst.com/

PPC SOFTWARE

http://www.adwordanalyzer.com/
http://www.adwordgenerator.com/
http://searchmarketingtools.com/ppc/ppcbidtracker.html

PPC TRAINING

If you're going to seriously compete in the cutthroat world of PPC advertising, I highly recommend you get Perry Marshall's book, *The Definitive Guide to Google AdWords*.

http://www.perrymarshall.com/adwords/

Besides driving online sales, PPC advertising can be used for lead generation and research by driving people to opt in and/or to survey pages. I also highly recommend Glenn Livingston's training material on conducting market research using search advertising coupled with surveys:

http://www.howtodoubleyourbusiness.com/

PPC INTELLIGENCE

Want to see the keywords your competitors are using? Or perhaps you'd like to see who's bidding on the same keywords you are. Check out these tools:

http://www.ispionage.com/
http://www.competitionequalizer.com/
http://www.affiliateelite.com/
http://www.spyfu.com/

PPC CAMPAIGN PERFORMANCE SOFTWARE

For detailed analysis of the PPC keyword performance for your site, consider these software tools:

http://www.xconversions.com/
http://www.keywordradar.com/

Payment Gateways and Payment Solutions

Payment gateways facilitate the movement of funds from the credit card networks to the bank account attached to your credit card merchant account.

If you're going to take credit card payments online using your own merchant account, you must also have an account with one of the payment gateways. While there are *many* others, four of the most popular follow.

PAYMENT GATEWAYS

http://www.authorizenet.com/
http://www.worldpay.com/
http://paypal.com/ (Payflow Pro or Website Payments Pro)
http://www.itransact.com/

THIRD-PARTY PAYMENT SOLUTIONS

If you don't have your own merchant account, you can still accept credit card orders online through one of these services:

http://www.2checkout.com/
http://www.paypal.com/
http://multicards.com/
http://www.propay.com/
http://www.cybersource.com/
http://www.otginc.com/integricharge.htm
http://www.ccnow.com/
http://alertpay.com/
http://www.paydotcom.com/

For digitally delivered products only, also consider these companies:

http://www.clickbank.com/
http://www.regsoft.com/
http://swreg.org/

PDF Resources

Adobe's Acrobat PDF file has become the most universally accepted method for exchanging documents, regardless of the platform used to create or read the document.

It used to be the only way to create or edit a PDF document was to purchase Adobe's Acrobat software—but not anymore! Since it became an ISO standard, a number of companies have created applications for PDF manipulation.

PDF CREATION

http://www.clicktoconvert.com/
http://www.pdfonline.com/
http://www.easysw.com/htmldoc/
http://www.ontheflypdf.com/
http://pdf995.com/
http://www.openoffice.org/

(Open Office is a complete business application suite that includes built-in PDF output features. Oh, and it's free.)

PDF CONVERTER

http://www.coolutils.com/Online-PDF-Converter.php

PDF STAMPING

http://www.verypdf.com/pdfstamp/
http://www.traction-software.co.uk/servertools/pdfimagestamp/
http://www.pdf-tools.com/asp/products.asp?name=BST

PDF EDITORS

http://www.adobe.com/
http://www.pdfill.com/
http://www.pdfhammer.com/
http://www.nitropdf.com/index.asp
http://www.nativewinds.montana.com/software/tomahawk
.html

Pop-Ups

Aside from other marketers, I don't believe I've ever heard anyone say good things about pop-ups—but the things keep on working like gangbusters.

Because of all the pop-up blockers, there's been a mass migration to using JavaScript and HTML layers to emulate a pop-up on the current web page. Technically these are not really pop-ups, because they don't open up a new window (the pop-up cannot be positioned outside the borders of the current window). Here are some resources for creating these new-generation pop-ups:

> http://www.marketingtips.com/hoverad/
> http://instantpopover.com/
> http://popover.generatorsoftware.com/
> http://www.dynamic-popup-generator.com/
> http://www.impactpopup.net/
> http://popup-toolkit.com/
> http://www.adimpact.com/ (hosted service)
> http://www.youcantblockthis.com/

One of the more recent breeds of pop-up is the *lightbox*.

With this style of pop-up, most of the page is grayed out, so the only "light" on the page focuses the visitor's attention on your desired message. This is powerful, but definitely something you'll want to test to make sure it's not just scaring your visitors away.

You can download free lightbox software from the download area of your reader rewards site:

http://www.LittleBlackBookRewards.com/

Podcasting/ Vidcasting

Imagine you have a weekly audio program that you record and upload to your web site as an MP3 file. You then send a little message to people on your e-mail list letting them know where they can go to download your latest broadcast.

Your subscribers go to the web page you have specified and download the MP3 file, then upload it into an iPod (or other MP3 player).

That's basically what podcasting is, but with one big difference. With podcasting, you don't need to do anything to inform your readers—they simply subscribe to an RSS feed, and their feed reader automatically downloads your audio broadcast as soon as you post it to your site. (If you don't know what RSS is, just skip ahead to the RSS section to get acquainted with it, then come back here.)

Look under "Audio" for tools to create your audio file.

PODCASTING RSS FEED GENERATORS

Once you have an audio file, you will need to create the RSS feed file. You can do this with the following software or services:

http://www.feedforall.com/
http://www.clickcaster.com/
http://www.libsyn.com/
http://www.myrsscreator.com/
http://www.softwaregarden.com/products/listgarden/
http://www.nightskyobserver.com/RSSGen/

PODCASTING WITH WORDPRESS

If you have a WordPress blog on your site, you can get a plug-in that enables you to publish your podcast directly from WordPress:

http://wordpress.org/extend/plugins/podcasting/

PODCAST DIRECTORIES

Once you create a podcast, you will want to submit it to some podcast directories:

http://www.digitalpodcast.com/
http://www.podcastdirectory.com/
http://www.podcastalley.com/
http://www.podcastpickle.com/

Also be sure to get an iTunes account and submit your podcast there:

http://www.itunes.com/

Note: You should know that iTunes is *not* just for music and video content!

VOICE-OVER SERVICES

If you want to have someone else record your podcast, check out these voice talent services:

http://www.voices.com/
http://voice123.com/
http://www.speedyspots.com/

VIDCASTING

Vidcasting is basically the same as podcasting, except you have video in addition to the audio. The only difference in the RSS file is that the enclosed file is a video file (with integrated audio) instead of audio.

If you want, you can enclose an audio file *and* a video file. That way, your subscribers can choose between one or the other—if they have only an audio-capable device, they can still listen to your broadcast.

ONE-STOP SERVICE SHOPS

These services are one-stop shops that allow you to create, publish, and distribute your podcasts and vidcasts all in one place:

http://www.hipcast.com/
http://www.audioacrobat.com/

Printing

With the cost of shipping things across the country these days, I honestly think you would be better off finding a local printer.

However if that's not possible, for whatever reason, there are some good companies to use.

ONLINE PRINTING SERVICES

http://www.kbp.com/
http://www.lelli.com/
http://www.nationalcolorcopy.com/defaults.asp
http://www.iprint.com/
http://www.48hrbooks.com/

Note the last one specializes in quick-turnaround book printing.

PRINT ON DEMAND

If you sell small quantities of information products, the print-on-demand model may make more sense than traditional printing and inventory storage.

These companies will print just a single copy of your product from a digital master, bind it according to your specification (perfect bound, spiral bound, etc.), and send it to your customers on demand.

It's certainly more expensive on a per-piece basis, but it's just so convenient that it may work better for you.

Another situation in which this would make sense is if your product is updated frequently—using print on demand, you will avoid having to recycle a pallet of unusable books when you come out with a new version.

Note that some of these companies will also duplicate CDs and DVDs for you in addition to printed material. Very cool.

http://www.Lulu.com/
http://www.cafepress.com/cp/info/sell/books.aspx
http://www.greenepublicationsinc.com/
http://mimeo.com/
http://www.printingforless.com/
http://www.vervante.com/
http://www.kunaki.com/ (just CDs and DVDs)

Project Management/ Groupware

Got a big project with many team members and resources to manage? This is for you. These online applications help you with team and resource management, issue tracking, scheduling, and more. These are quite powerful tools that you'll never want to do without once you've learned to use them.

http://www.basecamphq.com/
http://unfuddle.com/
http://phprojekt.com/index.php?&newlang=eng
http://www.activecollab.com/
http://www.clockingit.com/
http://crowdfavorite.com/products/
http://www.infowit.com/
http://quickbase.intuit.com/
http://goplan.info/
http://www.lighthouseapp.com/

Promotional Items and Incentives

These companies provide attention grabbers that you can employ in your direct response promotions.

MILLION DOLLAR BILLS

http://www.leadstampede.com/million-dollar-bills.htm

CHEAP CONSUMER ITEMS

http://www.dollardays.com/

GREAT BIG BALLS MAILED

http://www.sendaball.com/

OVERSIZED ITEMS

http://www.greatbigstuff.com/home.html

NOVELTY ITEMS

http://www.orientaltrading.com/

UNIQUE ATTENTION GRABBERS

http://impactproducts.net/

PERSONALIZED POKER CHIPS

http://www.homepokerchips.com/

FOREIGN MONEY

http://www.educationalcoin.com/

TRAVEL INCENTIVES

http://www.freevegas.com/
http://www.getupandgo.com/
http://www.sunrisepremiums.net/

Publicity

There are numerous stories of a successful publicity campaign giving a business owner exposure worth many thousand or even millions of dollars. Yes, this could even happen to you. However, even if you don't get the publicity home run, you can still benefit greatly from making consistent publicity efforts a permanent part of your marketing mix.

PUBLICITY TRAINING

Here are a few companies that specialize in publicity training and services:

http://www.rtir.com/
http://prprofits.com/
http://www.publicityinsider.com/
http://www.publicityhound.com/
http://www.directcontactpr.com/

PRESS RELEASE DISTRIBUTION SERVICES

If you're going to have someone in your organization take care of the publicity, here are some places where they can submit press releases:

http://www.xpresspress.com/
http://www.prweb.com/
http://www.pressreleasenetwork.com/
http://usanews.net/
http://www.businesswire.com/
http://www.ereleases.com/
http://www.eworldwire.com/
http://www.massmediadistribution.com/
http://www.24-7pressrelease.com/
http://www.empirenewswire.com/
http://www.free-press-release.com/
http://www.internetnewsbureau.com/
http://www.marketwire.com/mw/services_wiredistribution/
http://www.pressflash.com/
http://www.webwire.com/
http://www.prnewswire.com/

By the way, the submission of a press release is no longer *only* about attracting news organizations and magazine editors.

Even if you don't get any nibbles from the publishing world, you'll still get some play in the search engines for *each* of the stories you submit, and you'll even get some direct traffic from the online listings in the press release outlets themselves.

PRESS RELEASE DISTRIBUTION SOFTWARE

This software can be installed on a PC and will send out your press releases to the contacts you specify.

http://www.pressequalizer.com/

PRESS MEDIA GUIDES

If you want to narrowly target your publicity campaigns to publications in a specific industry, the following media guides will help you locate the relevant publications.

http://www.gebbieinc.com/
http://www.workshopinc.com/media2.htm
us.cision.com/products_services/bacons_media_
    directories_2009.asp

Really Simple Syndication (RSS)

An RSS feed is a summary of a news story, blog post, podcast, or some other kind of informational content.

For instance, most blog software will publish an RSS feed—this is just a file that is updated on the web site whenever a new post is submitted. Anyone who knows where to get the feed can then see the title (and some or even all of the content) for that new post.

The power of RSS is in the ability to subscribe to several RSS feeds through a feed reader. This way, you have central location where you can review the summaries of all the new content from all of the RSS feeds to which you are subscribed.

RSS READER SOFTWARE

The major browsers now have integrated RSS readers, but there are also some stand-alone readers that may have a richer feature set:

http://www.feedreader.com/
http://www.sharpreader.net/
http://www.rssreader.com/
http://www.newsgator.com/Individuals/FeedDemon/
http://www.newsgator.com/Individuals/NetNewsWire/
   (Mac OS X)

HOSTED RSS READERS

You can also have a Web-based (third-party-hosted) feed
reader just by signing up with one of these free services:

http://www.yahoo.com/
http://reader.google.com/
http://www.bloglines.com/
http://www.blogger.com/

This is all well and good, but how can you use RSS in
your business?

Well, RSS is used extensively by the social marketing
sites (see "Social Media Marketing" for more about that);
many of the social marketing methods and sites would not be
possible without RSS.

Beyond that, there's also a great deal of value in your
ability to get a continuous flow of fresh new content from
many sources.

This is great for research, but it is especially powerful
when integrated with your existing web site. With this constantly changing content, your site will be more attractive to
the search engines.

RSS DYNAMIC CONTENT

These resources will help you convert RSS feeds to dynamic content on your site:

http://www.rsstoblog.com/
http://www.dynaprime.com/
http://www.feedforall.com/more-php.htm

RSS DIRECTORIES

To locate RSS feeds related to the theme of your site, check out these resources:

http://www.syndic8.com/
http://www.rssfeeds.com/
http://www.rssmountain.com/rss_directory.php
http://www.magportal.com/

Also see "RSS Advertising" under "Advertising."

Referral Marketing Tools

The most effective form of advertising has always been word of mouth—someone is much more likely to purchase your product if it's been recommended by a friend. Internet technology has greatly increased the efficiency of referral marketing—people simply fill out an online form and click Send.

Not only that, but you can easily track the success of your referral marketing campaigns to see how many people have referred their friends, how many friends they referred, and even how many of those friends actually visited your site.

You can use a hosted service to implement a tell-a-friend function on your site:

http://www.supertaf.com/
http://www.tellafriendking.com/
http://www.tafmaster.com/

Or you could install software on your server. Before you do this, though, it's a good idea to check with your hosting company.

Since the software sends out e-mails from your server, there is the potential for abuse by your visitors: They could enter random e-mail addresses rather than e-mail addresses of their friends, and any resulting spam complaints would be traced back to your site. I haven't seen this happen, but it's always a possibility.

That being said, here are some server-based software solutions:

http://www.tafpro.com/ (Disclosure: I own this site.)
http://willmaster.com/master/recommend
http://www.viralfriendgenerator.com/
http://www.viralinviter.com/

This last one is one of the most recent tell-a-friend applications to come on the market, and it deserves special mention because of its "import" feature.

Rather than requiring your visitor to remember or copy/paste their "friend" e-mails into your tell-a-friend form, this software has an e-mail importer that grabs the e-mails straight from the sender's e-mail service.

Basically, senders enter their e-mail address and the password for their e-mail service (Yahoo!, Gmail, AOL, etc.), and this software logs into the e-mail system, grabs the sender's address book, and presents a list of names to the sender to choose from.

The sender then checks the box next to each of the people he or she wants to send the invitation to.

This feature greatly reduces the friction of filling out the form and results in a huge increase in the number of friends referred. Rather than the typical 3 to 5 friends, it's not uncommon to have the referral sent to 20 to 50 or more of the sender's friends!

One caveat, though: This may actually work *too* well. You need to be careful that you're not exceeding your server's capacity for sending e-mails, and you also want to make sure you aren't sending more e-mails than your hosting company allows.

If you have a very successful referral promotion and you're using *this* tool, you may find it necessary to move the software to a server dedicated exclusively to that task.

Research

The amount of information available on the Internet is a double-edged sword—it's an astonishing amount of information, to be sure, but it's easy to become overwhelmed when trying to analyze it and pull out any worthwhile conclusions.

Thankfully, a number of sites will happily grind through all the data for us. Using these tools, you can see what your competition is up to, find new niches (or more finely define your current ones), analyze key word relevance, spot consumer trends, and more.

SEARCH ENGINES

Usually, the first place we're going to start is the search engines. I know you *know* about these, but if I don't include them, someone is certain to write in their online book review, "What about Google?!"

Here are the major search engines:

http://www.google.com/
http://www.yahoo.com
http://www.msn.com
http://www.ask.com

http://www.gigablast.com
http://www.snap.com

METASEARCH ENGINES

These metasearch engines will simultaneously query several
search engines, remove the duplicates, and compile the results
for you . . . great for researching a topic.

http://www.ixquick.com/
http://dogpile.com/
http://www.metacrawler.com/
http://www.clusty.com/
http://www.surfwax.com/

METASEARCH SOFTWARE

There's also metasearch software for installation on your
computer:

http://www.copernic.com/
http://www.ferretsoft.com/

OTHER RESEARCH TOOLS

And here is some specialized search software that is highly
recommended:

http://www.searchautomator.com/

The Grokker site will group together concepts related to
your search value (keyword phrase). You can then click on

each group to drill down to more defined terms within that group. I personally drilled down nine levels deep on one of my searches. Pretty powerful.

http://www.grokker.com/

Yahoo! Answers can be the source of some extremely useful information that is difficult to find elsewhere:

http://answers.yahoo.com/

Assignment Editor is like a start page for news organizations—the search function doesn't impress me much, but it's still a good research tool because of the rich collection of resources listed:

http://www.assignmenteditor.com/

Here are a couple of good sites for searching online articles:

http://findarticles.com/
http://www.goarticles.com/

Looking for some fresh business ideas? Just browse at Springwise for a bit and you'll have all kinds of creative notions:

http://www.springwise.com/

For searching forum content, try these two sites:

http://www.boardtracker.com/
http://search.big-boards.com/

To find out what others have said about you or your product, check out the Googlism site:

http://www.googlism.com/

Search more than 150,000 magazines, journals, and newsletters here:

http://www.publist.com/

Jayde is a business-to-business (B2B) search engine—all sites have been human-reviewed before being included in the database:

http://www.jayde.com/

Sure, you have 10,000 bookmarks, but do you remember *why* you bookmarked each page? With this service, you can attach sticky notes to all sites of interest, reminding yourself what you found so useful:

http://www.mystickies.com/

Also check out the "Surfulator" software for saving and organizing your online research:

http://surfulator.com/

This site gives you a listing of different directories, along with the page rank value of each one. Getting a link from a high page rank directories will help your site's own page rank:

http://www.strongestlinks.com/directories.php

If you've ever wanted to see how a site has progressed over the years, you can view it in the Internet archive. Check out sites from 1996 for a good laugh!

http://www.archive.org

If you need to find the phone number for a business or individual, this is one of the better internet lookup services:

http://www.superpages.com/

Want to know when someone mentions your company? Want to know what they're saying about your competitors? Just set up an alert on one of these services and you'll receive an e-mail whenever a new mention is found.

http://www.webclipping.com/
http://googlealert.com/
http://www.google.com/alerts

If you want to be successful, you should *first* find out what people want and then sell it to them! These sites are great for figuring out what people are searching for and buying.

http://pages.ebay.com/sellercentral/whatshot.html
http://google.com/trends
http://50.lycos.com/
http://buzz.yahoo.com/overall/
http://www.amazon.com/gp/bestsellers/books/
http://asp.usatoday.com/life/books/booksdatabase/default
    .aspx
http://www.nytimes.com/pages/books/bestseller/

The world's largest marketplace is eBay, so give strong consideration to this eBay research tool:

http://www.auctionresearchtool.com

KEYWORD RESEARCH

http://www.nichemarketresearch.com/nf.php
http://www.wordtracker.com/
http://www.keywordelite.com/
http://keywordxray.com/

Microsoft has some interesting keyword search tools in its adLab:

http://adlab.msn.com/Keyword-Search.aspx
http://adlab.msn.com/OCI/oci.aspx

Also, get a Google AdWords account, which has a keyword tool that's fairly useful.

COMPETITIVE INTELLIGENCE

Sometimes you need to keep track of what your competitors are doing, and there are a number of sites that will help you obtain valuable competitive intelligence. These tools allow you to see what keywords they're using to advertise, their level of search engine saturation, which web sites are linking to them, when their pages change, and more.

http://www.alexa.com/
http://www.competitiondominator.com/
http://www.competitionequalizer.com/
http://www.googlealert.com/
http://www.ewatch.com/
http://www.cyberalert.com/
http://www.clippingservice.com/
http://www.marketleap.com/
http://www.nameintelligence.com/
http://www.spyfu.com/
http://www.affiliateelite.com/
http://trends.google.com/websites
http://www.compete.com/
http://keywordxray.com/
http://www.competitrack.com/

Screen Capture

It can be very useful to capture (record) your computer screen as you perform a specific task. That recording can become an instructional video or tutorial for your staff and/or clients, or perhaps a demo video to show to your prospects.

If all you need is a still image of your screen, you can do that without any special software, though the process is different for Windows and Mac computers.

For Windows, just press the "Print Screen" button on your keyboard (Windows PCs) and the current screen contents will be copied to your clipboard. You can then paste that into any graphics editor.

For your Mac, hit the Command (Apple) key, the Shift key, and the number 3 key simultaneously. This will save the current screen to the desktop as a PDF file. Or you can use the number 4 key, instead of 3, and that will allow you to select an area of the screen to capture to the PDF file.

Or (man, these Macs have a lot of options!) you can press the Control key at the same time as those listed above, and the screen will be captured to the clipboard, which you can then paste into a graphics program, email, or other document.

But what if you are trying to capture a web page that doesn't fit on one screen? The following screen capture tools have an option that can scroll the screen and capture the whole page as one long image. They also include some image manipulation and editing features.

http://www.techsmith.com/snagit.asp
http://www.faststone.org/FSCaptureDetail.htm
http://www.hyperionics.com/
http://www.etrusoft.com/screenshot-maker/index.htm

If you want to create a series of screen shots and arrange them into an instructional presentation, one way would be to capture all the screen shots and then import them into a PowerPoint presentation.

However, these software applications were designed specifically for building tutorials, and the resulting presentation looks almost like full-motion video.

http://www.debugmode.com/wink/
http://www.qarbon.com/presentation-software/viewletbuilder/

Sometimes only full-motion video will do, and if that's the case, you can use these applications.

http://www.techsmith.com/camtasia/
http://www.qarbon.com/presentation-software/vc/
http://www.etrusoft.com/screen-recorder/
http://www.camstudiopro.com/
http://www.camstudio.org/
http://jingproject.com/

This last one (Jing Project) is quite unique, because it automatically uploads your screen recording to its server and gives you a URL you can send to people for them to view the video. Quick and easy screen capture at it's best.

Jing Project and CamStudio.org are both free. I believe the others offer some additional features, but they may not be necessary for your presentation.

Note that full-motion video can result in very large files. If your target audience doesn't have high-bandwidth Internet connections, you may be better off using the Wink or Viewlet-Builder tutorial builders.

Search Engine Optimization

Search engine optimization (SEO) is something I just haven't been able to get into personally, but there's no question it's effective when done right.

Like everything else, there are two ways to approach it—do it yourself or pay someone else to do it.

SEO TRAINING

http://www.InternetMarketingSecrets.com/
http://www.undergroundtraininglab.com/
http://www.SearchNewz.com/
http://searchenginewatch.com/
http://www.bruceclay.com/
http://www.searchenginehelp.com/
http://www.highrankings.com/forum/
http://www.marketposition.com/
http://www.searchenginenews.com/
http://ezseonews.com/
http://www.seoprotoolz.com/

SEO SOFTWARE

If you decide to do it yourself, these software tools could come in handy:

http://www.seoelite.com/
http://www.optilinksoftware.com/

SEO SERVICES

There are tons of companies who will promise top-10 listings in the search engines, but "buyer beware" is an understatement. Here are four I feel safe in recommending:

http://www.netpost.com/
http://www.pageviews.com/home.htm
http://www.HighRankings.com/
http://www.searchenginehelp.com/

Security

I don't want to be an alarmist here, but whether for your office computer or your web server, security is critical—use it or risk losing everything.

COMPUTER SECURITY

To test your computer's vulnerability to intrusion from online sources, check out the "Shields Up" service at grc.com:

http://www.grc.com/

If the "Shields Up" service finds that your computer's ports are vulnerable, install some good firewall software. ZoneAlarm is one of the best:

http://www.zonelabs.com/

Antivirus software is critical as well. (These companies may also include firewall features, but I prefer to use ZoneAlarm.)

http://www.grisoft.com/doc/1/
http://www.avast.com/
http://www.mcafee.com/

SERVER SECURITY

One of the more common ways people hack into your web server is through unsecure web forms. For an explanation of how to test the web forms on your site, check out this article.

http://bontragerconnection.com/library/Form_Hijack_
    Testing.shtml

Also consider hiring the security services listed at the end of this section to do server "hardening."

PCI COMPLIANCE

If you are processing credit card payments on your site, you want to be especially careful that your server is not compromised. If you have your own merchant account and somebody hacks into your server and gains access to your customer's credit card numbers, you could be liable for huge fines.

To guard against this (and to absolve yourself of liability), you should make sure your server has Payment Card Industry (PCI) compliance, which is a standard set by the credit card companies to safeguard sensitive consumer information. These companies offer web server scanning services for PCI compliance.

http://www.ncircle.com/
http://www.hackerguardian.com/
https://www.controlscan.com/index.php
http://www.securityseer.com/

SECURITY SERVICES

Attaining PCI compliance can be a lengthy process, especially if the security scans reveal weaknesses in your system that must be resolved. If corrections must be made to your server configuration, you can enlist the services of these server management companies:

http://www.serverwizards.com/
http://www.platinumservermanagement.com/
http://www.easyservermanagement.com/

Shopping Cart Software/ Services

When you're preparing to take your business online, I believe the first decision you should make is which software you'll be using to run your online enterprise. If you're selling many items (which is typical of an e-commerce site), then one of the most critical questions you must answer is which shopping cart application to use.

Everyone's requirements are different, so I can't tell you which one is best for your company—but these are well known and reputable, and that will give you a good starting point for your own research.

SOFTWARE FOR UNIX/LINUX SERVERS

http://www.oscommerce.com/
http://www.shopsite.com/
http://www.mivamerchant.com/
http://www.eastland.com/carts.html

http://www.dansie.net/cart.html
http://www.fishcart.org/
http://www.avactis.com/
http://www.x-cart.com/
http://zencart.com/

SOFTWARE FOR WINDOWS SERVERS (ASP)

http://www.aspcart.com/
http://www.bvsoftware.com/
http://www.cart32.com/
http://www.cyberstrong.com/eshop/
http://www.ecommercesoft.net/

See also "E-commerce Integrated Systems" for additional cart solutions.

Software Marketing Tools

If you want to distribute free software or shareware, there are some special tools created just for you.

If your software is going to have a free-trial period, you can use this tool to integrate payment functions right in your application. The user can register your software (and pay for the registration) without ever leaving the application.

http://www.esellerate.net/

If you are distributing freeware or shareware, you can promote it through the software directories. To do this, you first need to create a *portable application description* (PAD) file. You can find a PAD-building tool here:

http://www.asp-shareware.org/pad/padgen.php

Once you have your PAD file, you can use PAD submission software to upload it to the software directories:

http://www.develab.net/
http://www.gsa-online.de/eng/softsubmit.html
http://www.dummysoftware.com/padexpress.html

Social Media Marketing

Social media differs from traditional media because the readers can participate in the creation of content by either adding content of their own or changing the existing content.

When most people hear the words "social media" or "social network," they think of MySpace and Facebook, but social media in its most basic form has been around long before these emerged.

For example, discussion boards (forums) have been on the Internet since 1996, and even before the World Wide Web existed, there were numerous bulletin board systems.

While it's true these didn't have the numerous social devices we have today, they still allowed people to form an interactive community based on a common interest—and isn't that what a social network is?

Social networks aren't the only kind of social media. You can share photos with Flickr and videos with YouTube without becoming part of a group or community there. These are nonetheless considered social media sites, because they're designed for the purpose of sharing and they allow viewer participation via comments.

Social media marketing generally has two goals:

1. *To gain exposure for your business.* This means you get out there in front of as many people as possible and give them great content and solutions. You don't market your products or services directly (though it's okay to let people know you have them); instead, you become the authority figure in your particular niche so people will think of you first when they have a need in that area.

2. *To provide links to your high-quality content pages for improved search engine listings.*

It's important to note that the content pages referred to in items 1 and 2 are *not* your main revenue-generating sites. They should have a single purpose, and that is simply to provide high-quality content to the reader.

These content pages don't sell your products or services, but they can have relevant links to your other sites that *do* sell—just make sure the content is valuable on its own and that the links are relevant to the topic.

As you use effective social marketing to promote these pages, they will rise to the top of the search engine listings for the keywords you are targeting. Since they will have links to your revenue-generating sites, those sites will be deemed more important by the search engines and will be displayed higher in the search listings.

Social marketing takes consistent effort and time, and it also requires some finesse. You must give high value to the network before you can expect anything in return.

Entire books have been written about social marketing tactics, but Michelle MacPhearson's "Social Media Daily Blueprint" has the most extensive resource listing I've seen and cuts right to the chase:

http://www.socialmediadaily.com/

This 26-page document gives you an outline of the pages where you can create content and the sites you can use to promote (bookmark) those content pages.

One warning: It's easy to feel intimidated when you see all the sites involved, and *yes*, it's a lot of work to begin with. However, it's probably the minimum amount of work required to get the kind of listings and traffic this work will produce.

I'd highly recommend outsourcing the bulk of the work after you have a good understanding of what's involved.

Another option is to let someone else handle the entire social marketing component of your business. These companies offer social marketing (also called *social media optimization*) services:

http://www.ebrandz.com/social-media-optimization.htm
http://www.socialmediapower.com/services/
http://www.brickmarketing.com/social-marketing-company
   .htm
http://www.convonix.com/social-media-optimization/

Though it won't have the long-term benefits of a properly executed social marketing campaign, another option (or something to consider in addition to your social marketing) is to advertise on the social networks.

These companies specialize in advertising in those channels:

http://www.socialmedia.com/
http://www.facebook.com/ads/
http://facebookcpanetwork.com/
http://www.cubics.com/

Spam

I have a friend who never had Internet service in her home until 2008.

Upon getting online, she quickly proceeded to sign up for a handful of free offers; as a result, within a week she had more than 2,000 spam e-mails. Ugh! I think she'll be getting a new e-mail address soon.

So, how do you fight the incessant bombardment to your in-box? For business owners, this is a tricky question, because if the controls you implement are too restrictive, you'll miss out on legitimate (and possibly critical) e-mails from your customers and business associates.

One of the first steps is to set up different e-mail addresses for different purposes, and then set up different spam countermeasures for each address.

You should have one e-mail address that you use only for personal correspondence. This should not be filtered in any way.

Create another e-mail address for your customers. Unless you start seeing some abuse, you shouldn't filter this e-mail address, either. (Also, consider giving customers a link to your help desk page instead of an e-mail address.)

Never use the aforementioned e-mail addresses when you're signing up for newsletters, e-zines, or autoresponders of any kind. Don't use them when you place an online order. For those functions, have a different e-mail address—this one will be filtered aggressively.

When I speak of *filtering*, I'm talking about using the antispam features of your e-mail software. Most e-mail clients have this, and you can tweak the settings to be more or less aggressive. The more restrictive your filters, the more false positives you'll get.

Often, when you place an order or sign up for a newsletter, the order confirmation e-mail will be shunted to your spam or junk folder by your e-mail client—so always check there before complaining to the merchant that you didn't get an e-mail receipt.

If your e-mail client doesn't include filtering features, this service may be used instead:

http://www.filtermy.com/home.shtml

There are a number of "challenge-response" e-mail services, and some ISPs also provide this feature for no additional charge.

These work by sending an automatic "challenge" e-mail to anyone who sends you an e-mail. If that person receives the challenge and responds in the specified manner (clicks on a link or types the right word in a box), then the e-mail is sent on to you.

If the sender never responds, you never see the e-mail. Once people respond, they will be white-listed and will not be challenged again—their future e-mails will sail right through.

This will dramatically cut down on your incoming spam—in fact, it may eliminate it altogether. However, most automatic e-mails from order or subscription processes will also be blocked, so I'd recommend using a challenge-response system only for your personal e-mail address.

http://www.spamarrest.com/
http://www.blockallspam.com/
http://www.cleanmymailbox.com/

These services will allow you to check the "Subject" and "From" lines of your incoming e-mail before it leaves your server. You can delete any obvious spam without ever down-loading the e-mail to your own system. This can be especially useful if you have a slow Internet connection.

http://www.eremover.bizhosting.com/
http://www.crystaloffice.com/msinfo.html
http://www.mailwasher.net/

Split Testing Services/ Software

To realize the maximum possible response rate to your advertisements and sales pages, their various components should be tested on a continual basis. Some of the things you should test include:

Offer (what customers get for their money)
Price and payment options
Headlines (including super- and subheadlines)
Body copy
Fonts used in the headlines and body copy
Background page color
Header image—including using no header at all
Different graphics and different captions for them
Subject lines in e-mails
"From" header in e-mails
Text or HTML e-mail
Long or short copy
Inclusion or exclusion of audio or video
Layout of the page

The simplest way to test the effectiveness of each of these elements is to perform a series of A/B split tests, which work in the following manner: You direct incoming traffic to two different pages that are identical except for the single thing you're testing. After you get a statistically valid number of conversions (30 to 50) from each page, you pick the winner.

Once you have a winner, you use the winning page as the control and set up another page to test some other change. Then go back to step 1 and repeat.

These software packages will manage the split testing for you:

http://www.splitanalyzer.com/
http://www.splittestaccelerator.com/free_mvt_course.php
http://www.l-space-design.com/Products/Conversion_
  Booster.aspx

The problem with the traditional A/B split test is that it's serial in nature—you test one thing at a time and wait for the results of that test before moving on to the next test subject.

With multivariate testing, you don't have this limitation. You can test many things at once and find out which combination of various components will offer the best conversion rates. These companies provide software you can install on your own server to do multivariate testing:

http://www.phpzen.com/split-run-test/
http://www.splittestaccelerator.com/

http://www.kaizentrack.com/
http://www.conversiondoubler.com/

If you prefer, you can use a hosted solution (both A/B and multivariate testing) offered by these companies:

http://www.vertster.com/
http://www.offermatica.com/
http://www.optimost.com/
http://www.google.com/websiteoptimizer

Note: In the case of Google's free service, I don't think "you get what you pay for" applies—it's awesome!

Survey Services/ Software

Surveys may be one of the most underutilized weapons in the business owner's arsenal. You can use them to determine which product you should release next and how much to charge for it. They can also be used to find the various segments of your market, to identify hot prospects, and more.

HOSTED SURVEY SERVICES

Hosted survey services generally work by giving you a small snippet of HTML code to add to your site, or a link to include in an e-mail. You can start/stop a survey and view the survey results in an online control panel. There are a number of companies to choose from:

http://www.surveygizmo.com/
http://www.surveymonkey.com/
http://www.mrpoll.com/
http://www.zoomerang.com/

http://www.HostedSurvey.com/
http://polldaddy.com/
http://www.createsurvey.com/
http://www.oneminutepoll.com/
http://www.askdatabase.com/

SURVEY SOFTWARE

If you'd rather have full control and exclusive access to your data, you can install one of these survey software applications on your server:

http://www.willmaster.com/master/survey/
http://www.chumpsoft.com/
http://sourceforge.net/projects/phpesp/
http://www.beachtech.com/

The Beach Tech software is unique in that it produces surveys you can send in an e-mail. The respondents simply send an e-mail back, and the results are tabulated by the software. It would be interesting to see how many more (or less!) people would actually respond to the survey if they could do it without leaving their e-mail address.

For advanced training on how to use surveys in your marketing research, I highly recommend Glenn Livingston's course, offered at the following web site:

http://www.howtodoubleyourbusiness.com/

Livingston has repeatedly demonstrated the ability to enter new markets with virtually no risk with these market research methods.

If you're already in a market, these methods will help you find out what your customers really want and potentially double your business with that new knowledge.

Livingston puts it like this:

> I'm talking about doing a thorough and complete A to Z research project that covers every aspect of the market and provides you with a detailed list of exactly what your market is looking for, what they'll be most likely to pay for, exactly how much it should cost you to generate a sale *(down to the penny!)*, and how to break your market into smaller groups for maximum effectiveness.

Again, highly recommended.

Tracking

Most direct response marketing experts share a common mantra: "Test everything." However, testing something is meaningless if you can't track the results. Fortunately for all of us, tracking is an inherent property of Internet technology—just about anything can be tracked.

What specific metrics should the prudent online business owner be tracking? For starters, you'll want to track the performance of your advertising.

You'll need to know the number of visitors, number of registrations (subscribers to any opt-in lists), and number of sales resulting from each advertising campaign. From this you can also determine the cost and revenue per visitor.

Armed with this knowledge, you can make an informed decision about whether to terminate or increase spending for each traffic source.

One bit of advice: You may find that some traffic sources result in an initial loss. However, if you know that the average lifetime value of a customer greatly exceeds the cost of obtaining that customer, it may be in your best interest to continue advertising in that channel.

Of course, you'll want to optimize your process—ideally, you can turn the front-end loss into a break-even situation or even a profit.

AD TRACKING SERVICES

Here, then, are several hosted services for tracking your online advertising campaigns:

http://www.clickalyzer.com/
http://www.conversionruler.com/
http://www.clickpath.com/

AD TRACKING SOFTWARE

If you want to do it all in-house, you can install some software on your web server to handle the tracking:

http://www.adtrackz.com/
http://www.visitorville.com/
http://www.dynatracker.com/
http://sitesupertracker.com/
http://www.prolinkz.com/
http://www.extremetracking.com/
http://www.covertconversionpro.com/

WEB TRAFFIC TRACKING

In addition to tracking the performance of your advertising campaigns, it can be enlightening to examine the general movement of your web site visitors.

Among other things, you can see where they're coming from, the search terms they used to find your site in the search engines, what pages they are visiting and how long they're staying on your site.

http://www.google.com/analytics/
http://www.hypertracker.com/
http://www.superstats.com/
http://www.extremetracking.com/
http://www.statcounter.com/

KEYWORD TRACKING

Some of the most valuable intelligence you can obtain is the performance of the keywords you are bidding on in the pay-per-click search engines. These applications will give you an X-ray view:

http://www.keywordradar.com/
http://www.xconversions.com/
http://keywordxray.com/

See also "Split Testing Services/Software."

Video

With worldwide broadband access approaching 240 million subscribers (see oecd.org/sti/ict/broadband), the addition of video to your site has entered the realm of practicality.

However, since that represents roughly a sixth of total Internet subscribers, you should still design your site such that your low-bandwidth visitors are not excluded.

This means your site should be able to convey your message even if none of the video components are activated, or you should supply low-bandwidth alternatives. Simply reducing the size and bit rate of your video can reduce its download time by a factor of 10.

You should definitely test how video content and bandwidth requirements affect your sales conversion rate.

The first step in adding video to your site is, of course, to produce the video. Depending on the purpose of your video, this can be a live recording or a full-motion screen capture.

For live recordings, the simplest method is to use either a digital camera with a movie mode or a webcam.

SIDE NOTE

For professional-quality production, you'll need more sophisticated equipment, including a camera, lighting, and possibly a green screen setup. I refer you to Perry Lawrence at www.askmrvideo.com for those kinds of questions.

See "Screen Capture" for full-motion screen capture resources.

VIDEO EDITING SOFTWARE

Once you have a video, you can optionally dress it up by adding background music, transitions, text overlays, and so on. Windows and Mac both come with free software (Windows Movie Maker and iMovie, respectively) for doing this. Or you can get a commercial application:

http://ulead.com/vs/runme.htm
http://www.adobe.com/products/premiereel/
http://www.sonycreativesoftware.com/products/vegas
    family.asp

Using movie software, you can also integrate animation sequences in your video (see "3D Rendering and Animation Software" under "Graphics").

VIDEO CONTENT SOURCES

You can get royalty-free video content (transitions, background footage, etc.) from several content providers. These add professionalism and zing to your final product:

http://www.digitaljuice.com/
http://www.artbeats.com/
http://www.footagefirm.com/
http://www.animationsforvideo.com/
http://www.videocopilot.net/
http://www.revostock.com/
http://www.motionloops.com/
http://www.motiongraphicslab.com/

You can also get background music for your videos—review resources in the "Audio" section.

WEB-VIDEO TOOLS

Once you have a video exactly the way you want it, you'll need to convert it to a Web-friendly format, and several software applications do a nice job of this:

http://www.msiwebvideo.com/
http://www.flvproducer.com/
http://www.easywebvideo.com/
http://www.swishzone.com/index.php?area=products
&product=video

Another option is to use camdeo.com, with which you can make videos using just your webcam and computer microphone.

http://www.camdeo.com

Sometimes you may find it necessary to convert between different video formats (WMV to MPEG4, AVI to MOV, etc.)—see "File Format Conversion" for some tools to do this.

VIDEO DISTRIBUTION SERVICES

An added benefit of having video on your site is that you can submit that video to video sharing sites and get links back to your site from them. This will result in some direct traffic to your site, but more important, it will help your site get more play in the search engines.

To save time (it takes a while to upload video files), you can use one of the several video distribution services:

http://www.trafficgeyser.com/
http://www.tubemogul.com/
http://heyspread.com/

VIDEO SPOKESPERSON SERVICES

You may want to deliver a short presentation from a real person, but prefer not to do it yourself—maybe you're camera, shy, or perhaps you just don't want to mess with the technical aspects of getting it done.

Several companies now offer "video spokesperson" services. They employ professional actors (including actual broadcast television and radio talent, in many cases), and they produce the video for you. There's no quicker or easier way to get a professional-quality video presentation on your site.

Generally, these companies are promoting packages containing anywhere from 15 to 90 seconds of video footage, but they can do longer presentations if required:

http://www.livefaceonweb.com/
http://www.peopleonyourpage.com/
http://www.livepersonality.com/
http://www.persononweb.com/
http://websitetalkingheads.com/
http://www.spokespersoncenter.com/
http://www.ispokesperson.com/
http://www.videospokespeople.com/
http://www.videohotshots.com/

VIRTUAL CHARACTER SERVICES

You can also have virtual characters on your web site. Though they're obviously not real people, they can still grab and focus your visitors' attention.

http://www.oddcast.com/sitepal/
http://www.mediasemantics.com/

VIRTUAL CHARACTER SOFTWARE

There's also software that does this, and not just with human characters, but animals as well. These can be put to good use if your site is more casual in nature (and, in my opinion, this would be excellent for sites catering to younger audiences):

http://www.reallusion.com/crazytalk/default.asp

Because video is high-bandwidth content, consider the resources under "Media Hosting."

Viral Marketing

The definition of *viral marketing* depends on whom you're asking, but the one I like is "marketing phenomenon which facilitates and encourages people to pass along a marketing message" (see marketingterms.com).

The idea in its simplest form is that you create something (a product, a video, a social networking widget) so compelling that people *want* to pass it along to others. You also supply a mechanism that makes it easy for them to pass it along.

What makes it compelling? It may be something humorous, like a funny video, or something really unusual, cool, or wacky. It could be compelling because there's a reward for passing it along (e.g., "Pass this on to three friends and we'll give you a free ringtone")—though that's not as powerful as something that's just really *fun* or *cool*.

Your viral marketing can be especially effective if the marketing message is passed along simply by using your product. Here are some examples:

> Hotmail includes a link to its service at the bottom of every outgoing e-mail. You simply *use* Hotmail to send e-mails and its marketing message is passed along with no additional effort on your part.

At the end of every YouTube video, the viewer is invited to send it to a friend. By simply using the video service to embed video on your site, you're also promoting it.

Google has an "Ads by Google" link in the AdSense ads displayed throughout the Internet. When you monetize your site with its ads, you're also promoting its service.

Several companies provide free web site templates that you can download and use for your own site. At the bottom of each page is a link to the template site. This not only results in direct traffic, but also helps the template site in the search engines.

To get started with viral marketing in its simplest form, find something with a high perceived value that you can give away—and give people a good reason to pass it along to others.

VIRAL PDF E-BOOKS

One example of a common strategy is to release a PDF e-book that you sell for a low price or simply give away. You give your customers the rights to sell or give away a version of the e-book that has been branded with their web site address.

At first glance, it seems like this would be a terrible idea! However, for you, the e-book is serving as a sales brochure. It contains some good, solid information, and it has value to the reader by itself—while also promoting your main product.

Now, what would induce your customers to distribute this e-book? Typically, it's one or more of the following:

- The e-book is branded with their web site address, so they can promote it as a way to draw visitors to their site.
- If you offer high-quality information, they may distribute it just for the goodwill it generates toward them and their business.
- If you have their affiliate link for your main product in the e-book, then they will receive a commission for any sales generated by the distributed e-book.

For creating this kind of branded PDF e-book, check out the following sites:

http://viralpdf.com/
http://www.ontheflypdf.com/
http://viraldocumenttoolkits.com/
http://www.affiliate-pdf-brander.com/

The viral e-book idea is old (as the Internet goes), but still effective if done right. At the very least, consider providing your affiliates with branded e-books they can use for lead generation.

VIRAL LIST BUILDER

A more recent twist on this idea is to maintain control of the distribution, but let other people keep 100 percent of the sales price sent directly to their PayPal account.

Since you're selling an e-book (or other digitally delivered product), this method allows you to quickly build a sizable customer list with virtually no cost. Here's how it works:

1. People purchase your product.
2. After the purchase, they fill out a simple registration form that adds them to your list and gives them access to the download page (this can be automated).
3. On the download page, they are invited to tell others about your product, for which they will receive 100 percent of the sale price sent directly to their PayPal account.
4. They copy a special link you provide and send it to their list.
5. When people on their list purchase, the money is sent directly to the referring party's own PayPal account.
6. The new customer is automatically redirected to the registration form on *your* site, and you start again at step 2.

This works well for two reasons. First, you are giving people strong incentive—immediate financial gain (all the money)—to promote your product.

Second, you have removed all the difficult technical obstacles: They aren't required to set up a web site or payment system, and they don't even need to register as an affiliate—they merely copy a web link and send it to their list.

Adding a "tell a friend" script on the customer thank-you page can magnify the power of this method if your customers aren't likely to have marketing lists of their own. See "Referral Marketing Tools" for more about these.

Take note that the list you're building with this method is not an average run-of-the-mill "free download" list. This is a list of people who have actually *paid money online for your product,* which is orders of magnitude better than any "free download" or "free newsletter" list.

Jonathan Leger's popular software script for implementing this strategy on your own site can be purchased for just $7.00:

http://www.the7dollarsecrets.com/

One caveat to consider—refer to step 5 above—the problem with this for the referring party is that they are on the hook if you don't deliver the product. Make sure you give excellent customer support or nobody will want to put their PayPal account on the line to promote your products.

WIDGETS FOR VIRAL MARKETING

The popularity of social networks greatly amplifies the viral potential of anything you do there. Now, with the click of a button, a whole network of friends can be exposed to your message.

This isn't in-your-face advertising, though. Rather, you create a widget—something that's useful or funny and that people will want to share—and make it available for people to add to their own web pages (including, but not limited to, their social network pages).

Your product is not the focus of the widget, but it can be associated with the component. For instance, if you sell a "low-calorie cooking" book, you might supply a "Calorie Estimator" widget or perhaps a "Daily Low-Cal Menu" widget. At the bottom of the widget, you'd have a low-key "Sponsored by" or "More recipes . . ." link to your site.

The widget is just a snippet of HTML or JavaScript code that pulls content from your web server and displays it on the user's web site.

Here are some services that simplify the creation and distribution of widgets:

http://www.clearspring.com/
http://www.widgetbox.com/
http://sproutbuilder.com/
http://www.musestorm.com/
http://www.iwidgets.com/

This site looks especially helpful if you want to maximize your distribution and sharing capabilities:

http://www.gigya.com/

Google has its own engine for creating widgets, but it calls them *gadgets*. To create your own Google gadgets, which can be placed on any web page, check out this page:

http://code.google.com/apis/gadgets/docs/legacy/dev_ guide.html

To get some ideas from existing gadgets, go here:

http://www.google.com/ig/directory?synd=open

SIDE NOTE

It's easy to become confused when looking for information regarding widgets. The widgets I'm talking about here are designed to be added to any web page, *not* to your local computer desktop and *not necessarily* to a social network page (though they can be).

Google has two different kinds of web *gadgets* (Google's name for widgets). The preceding links point to Google's "legacy" web gadgets, which will work on any web page.

Google also has a new kind of gadget designed to work with the OpenSocial API (discussed later)—these gadgets can be added only to web sites that have implemented the "OpenSocial API Specification." Unless you're running your own social network, chances are slim that OpenSocial is available on your site.

Google also has gadgets designed for its "Google Desktop" application, which you can install on your computer. To create this kind of "Google Desktop" widget, check out this site:

http://desktop.google.com/plugins/

Yahoo! has something similar that it calls *widgets* (confused yet?), which can be deployed to your desktop but not to a web page.

(Continued)

> If you're interested in creating this kind of widget (for deployment to your customer's local desktop, not to a web page), check out these resources:
>
> http://widgets.yahoo.com/
> http://widgetworld.com/

VIRAL SOCIAL NETWORK APPLICATIONS

In terms of viral potential, social network applications are the next step up from widgets. Applications differ from widgets in that they have access to the core social functions of the network.

For example, a Facebook application can access the news feed, make requests, and share functions, among other tasks.

This is very powerful from a viral standpoint, because it means the entire "friend" network of those using your application can be exposed to its existence and invited to use it and/or install it on their own page.

Network applications were first introduced by Facebook, but Google is now promoting a standard implementation of network applications called OpenSocial. This standard has been adopted by several social networks, though not by Facebook.

For converting your widgets to Facebook applications, check out these two sites:

http://www.clearspring.com/platform/facebook
http://docs.widgetbox.com/developers/app-accelerator/

These companies offer OpenSocial-based application development services:

http://www.contextoptional.com/
http://momentumdesignlab.com/services/social_media.php

YOUR OWN SOCIAL NETWORK

If you want to start your own social network, a number of companies provide the necessary platforms for doing so. Here are a few:

http://www.ning.com/
http://www.kickapps.com/
http://www.onesite.com/
http://www.neeetz.com
http://www.collectivex.com/

This would be the ultimate in viral marketing (assuming you are able to reach a critical mass of users), because everyone who brings a friend into the community is also promoting your social network.

Web Design Resources

You could fill a small library with the books and articles that have been written about web design. If you have any inclination to do web design (or have someone in your company do it), these resources will get you started.

Additional resources (an overwhelming number!) are readily available online.

WEB SITE TEMPLATES

Sometimes you want to put a site up quickly. You don't have time for a custom design, but you still want it to look nice. Templates sites are perfect for this situation.

Just pick the template you like, pull it into your web design application, and add your copy and images. If you can't find anything you like on these sites, there are many more; simply do a Google search for "web site templates."

http://www.basictemplates.com/
http://www.freesitetemplates.com/
http://www.1000webtemplates.com/
http://laughingbird.com/

http://www.freesitetemplates.com/
http://ezminisites.com/

WEB DESIGN TUTORIALS

If you want to learn or brush up on web design principles, check out these tutorial pages:

http://www.w3schools.com/
http://boogiejack.com/html_tutorials.html
http://htmlgoodies.com/
http://reference.sitepoint.com/
http://www.htmlgoodies.com/beyond/dhtml/index.php

HTML VALIDATION

This service will validate the code that makes up your site, informing you of any detected errors:

http://www.w3schools.com/site/site_validate.asp

To verify that your site is viewable in different kinds of browsers, use browsershots.org—it will create snapshots of your site as viewed from various browsers:

http://browsershots.org/

FAVICON GENERATOR

A favorites icon, or *favicon* ("fav icon") is the little picture that shows up next to some of the sites in your bookmarks or favorites listing. All you need to do is upload a "favicon.ico" to your web site's web folder and it will appear next to your site URL when people come to your site.

This utility helps you to create a correctly formatted favicon.ico file:

http://www.favicongenerator.com/

INTERACTIVE SALES LETTERS

The contents of an interactive sales letter will change as the reader selects different options—thus, you can emphasize features of your product that correspond to the selections the visitor has made.

http://www.interactivesalesletter.com/

WEB FORMS

These services make web forms (the kind your visitors fill out and submit) easy to implement on your site.

http://www.responders.com/
http://www.response-o-matic.com/
http://www.logiforms.com/
http://www.formlog.com/
http://www.formsite.com/
http://www.freedback.com/

WEB DESIGN SOFTWARE

Web design software comes in two basic flavors: HTML editors and "What You See Is What You Get" (WYSIWYG) editors. With the WYSIWYG editors, it's almost like using your favorite word processor—you don't need to know any HTML code.

One drawback is that some of them add extraneous HTML code to your page, or make undesired changes to special characters or sometimes even to your live web site pages. Most of this can be controlled by setting the options correctly.

The de facto standard in web design software is Adobe Dreamweaver:

http://www.adobe.com/products/dreamweaver/

There are a lot of other good choices, though, including several high-quality free applications, a few of which follow.

HTML EDITORS

These editors will help you to create web sites at the code level. They're not as simple as the WYSIWYG editors, but these can come in handy at times when you need to do a little streamlined HTML

http://www.coffeecup.com/freestuff/ (free)
http://www.evrsoft.com/1stpage2.shtml (free)

http://www.arachnoid.com/arachnophilia (free)
http://www.kevingunn.com/ (Web-O-Rama)

WYSIWYG EDITORS

"What You See Is What You Get" editors make web page creation as simple as using your word processor, though sometimes the code is not as clean as what you'd get using an HTML editor. Still, from the end-user perspective there's usually no observable difference.

http://www.xsitepro.com/
http://www.coffeecup.com/html-editor/
http://www.123wysiwyg.com/
http://www.evrsoft.com/1stpage3.shtml
http://www.mcwebsoftware.com/wwez (free)
http://freeserifsoftware.com/software/WebPlus/default.asp
http://www.webpage-maker.com/
http://www.webstudio.com/

ONLINE WYSIWYG EDITORS

There are also some services that allow you to build your site through an online drag-and-drop interface (no software to download, just use your web browser):

http://business.blinkweb.com/
http://www.sitegalore.com/
http://www.wix.com/

Many web hosting accounts include "site builder" tools, so if you already have a web site, be sure to check for this kind of feature in your hosting account's control panel.

The "turnkey web store" solutions discussed later in this section also include browser-based site design and editing functions.

Marlon Sanders's product is . . . well, different. But this section feels like the most logical place to include it. Definitely check it out.

http://www.designdashboard.com/

WEB SITE EDITING SOFTWARE

Web site editing software is different from the preceding web design packages because it's not really design software; it's "quick edit" software.

After you install it on your web server, anyone you give the password to can make change on your site with only his or her web browser.

http://www.flypage.com/
http://www.editize.com/
http://www.interspire.com/webedit/

Web Hosting Services

Most businesses will have their web sites hosted at a hosting company. These companies maintain the servers and Internet connection, and you simply upload files to put them online.

The two main server platforms for which 99 percent of available software is designed are Unix/Linux and Microsoft Windows. Most web hosting companies can set you up with either platform. In my experience there is more software written for Unix/Linux web servers, so all other things being equal, that's what I'd recommend.

Before you make any decisions regarding web hosting, you should know what software you'll be running—different server platforms are required depending on the software you'll be using. In some cases you can get a version of the software to run on Unix/Linux or a different version for Windows, but quite often the software is only available for one or the other.

SHARED HOSTING

The most common form of web hosting is *shared* hosting, which means your site shares resources with several other sites.

The web hosting companies have resource allocation software in place to make sure nobody crashes the server with a rogue script or huge traffic spike, but you still won't get the maximum performance that's available with a dedicated server.

Many hosting companies will promote something called a *virtual private server* (VPS). This is still shared hosting, but you have a higher level of flexibility and control over the system.

The following shared hosting services all have good reputations for reliability and support—I've used more than half of them myself, and the others have been recommended by people I trust:

http://www.lunarpages.com
http://www.hostdepartment.com/
http://www.hostmonster.com/
http://www.hostgator.com/
http://www.pair.com/
http://www.1and1.com/
http://www.alabanza.com/
http://www.mewebhost.com/
http://www.siteworks.com/
http://www.servint.net/
http://www.isitebuild.com/sitehosting.htm
http://www.kiosk.ws
http://www.thirdspherehosting.com/

http://www.site5.com/
http://maxnethosting.com/

DEDICATED HOSTING

Once your hosting requirements exceed the resources available with shared hosting, you'll need to get a dedicated server, with all of the server's resources dedicated exclusively to your site(s).

This is my short list of high-performance dedicated server providers at reasonable cost. I've used every one of these for my own sites or my clients' sites, and they are all superb in terms of reliability and support response time and competence.

http://www.fastservers.com/
http://www.rackspace.com/
http://www.theplanet.com/
http://www.1and1.com/
http://www.servint.net/

E-COMMERCE STORE HOSTING

Depending on what you're doing on the Internet, you may not need a traditional hosting account.

If you're running an e-commerce store, the services offered by some of the bigger store providers may be sufficient for your needs:

http://prostores.com/index.html
http://smallbusiness.yahoo.com/
http://www.volusion.com/
http://www.zoovy.com/
http://order.1and1.com/xml/order/Eshops
http://pages.ebay.com/storefronts/start.html

Web Site Monitoring

Don't wait for a prospective customer to alert you to a problem with your site. The tools listed here allow you to monitor one or more web sites, and they will notify you when any of the following occur:

- Site goes down.
- Performance degrades.
- Incoming links change.
- Content changes.
- Security vulnerabilities are detected.

Some offer more features than others, so check them all out to see which one meets your requirements best.

http://www.alertra.com/
http://www.netwhistle.com/
http://www.cyberspyder.com/linkservice.html
http://watchdog.superstats.com/
http://www.alertmefirst.com/
http://www.tracerlock.com/

http://www.updatepatrol.com/
http://www.seventwentyfour.com/
http://www.alertsite.com/ (includes load testing feature)
http://www.internetseer.com/
http://www.dotcom-monitor.com/

Your Reader Rewards Site

This was mentioned in the introduction, but it's important enough to repeat it at the end of this book . . .

Because things change so rapidly online, I have created a web site just for owners of this book. Please enter this web address in your browser:

http://www.LittleBlackBookRewards.com/

Registration is free and will give you access to additional resource links, free downloadable software, and more.

Index